COLLECTOR'S
VALUE GUIDE™

NASCAR®
Die-Cast Collectibles

Collector Handbook
and Price Guide

PREMIERE EDITION

NASCAR® Die-Cast Collectibles

EDITORIAL

Managing Editor: Jeff Mahony
Associate Editors: Melissa A. Bennett, Jan Cronan, Gia C. Manalio, Paula Stuckart
Contributing Editor: Mike Micciulla
Assistant Editors: Heather N. Carreiro, Jennifer Filipek, Joan C. Wheal
Editorial Assistants: Jennifer Abel, Timothy R. Affleck, Beth Hackett, Christina M. Sette, Steven Shinkaruk

WEB
(CollectorsQuest.com)

Web Reporter: Samantha Bouffard
Web Graphic Designer: Ryan Falis

R&D

R&D Specialist: Priscilla Berthiaume
R&D Graphic Designer: Angi Shearstone

ART

Creative Director: Joe T. Nguyen
Assistant Art Director: Lance Doyle
Senior Graphic Designers: Susannah C. Judd, David S. Maloney, Carole Mattia-Slater, David Ten Eyck
Graphic Designers: Jennifer J. Bennett, Sean-Ryan Dudley, Kimberly Eastman, Marla B. Gladstone, Melani Gonzalez, Caryn Johnson, Jaime Josephiac, James MacLeod, Jeremy Maendel, Chery-Ann Poudrier

PRODUCTION

Production Manager: Scott Sierakowski
Product Development Manager: Paul Rasid

ISBN 1-58598-069-2

306 Industrial Park Road
Middletown, CT 06457
CollectorsQuest.com

Table Of Contents

Welcome To The World Of NASCAR®

Once known as "the sport of the South," NASCAR® has exploded into a nationwide phenomenon. Its enormous appeal is evident, as skyrocketing television ratings have shown races to be among the most popular televised events today.

The *Collector's Value Guide™ to NASCAR® Die-Cast Collectibles* is your comprehensive source for understanding both the sport itself and the popular line of collectibles it has inspired. Here you can find the most up-to-date information on die-cast collectibles for nine of the hottest drivers in the sport today, including Jeff Burton, Dale Earnhardt®, Jeff Gordon®, Dale Jarrett®, Bobby Labonte™, Mark Martin®, Tony Stewart®, Rusty Wallace® and rookie Dale Earnhardt Jr.

In addition to full-color photos of each car, we will give you all of the applicable manufacturers and scales for that paint scheme – all in one easy to use format. Finally, we list secondary market prices for each to help you determine the value of your collection.

So, whether you are new to the sport of NASCAR or you have been a die-hard fan for years, this guide is the book for you! Look inside for other great features including:

- **Bios for the nine racers included in this book, as well as fan club information**
- **A history of how stock car racing became the powerhouse sport it is today**
- **A guide to all of the tracks in the Winston Cup Series**
- **A look at great racers and great moments in racing from years past**
- **And much, much more!**

The History Of NASCAR®

Stock-car racing got its start on the dirt roads of the rural Southeast. In pre-NASCAR days, the woods were dotted with hidden stills used in the production of corn whiskey, commonly known as moonshine. Special cars with souped-up engines helped the bootleggers outrun the Feds and successful drivers/distillers became local folk heroes. Sometimes the bootleggers would race against each other and these loosely organized and locally promoted dirt-track races eventually evolved into the phenomenon that is NASCAR.

Bill France & The Birth Of NASCAR®

Back in the early days of NASCAR, there were many organizations billing themselves as sanctioning bodies of the sport. It seemed that every organization had its own champions, standards and rules and those were just from the *legitimate* organizations. Many more races were run by unscrupulous promoters who overlooked flagrant cheating by popular drivers, advertised huge prizes that didn't exist and frequently sneaked away while a race was in progress, taking all the ticket money with them.

Between the moonshine runners and the crooked promoters, racing seemed doomed to be an outlaw sport forever. It was against this cultural backdrop that William Henry Getty France, or "Big Bill" as he was known, got his start. France was an expert mechanic and racer who moved his family from Washington, D.C. to Daytona Beach, Florida in 1934. Daytona already had a long history as a racing town; in the early days of the automobile, many land speed records were set on Daytona's long, flat beaches. As the speeds grew higher, the record-setting action moved from Daytona and the Daytona Chamber of Commerce, hoping to keep the race tourists, set up a 4.1 mile course on the beach. The first two races held on this course, in 1936 and 1937, were far from organized, so in 1938, France was given the opportunity to organize the race. He attracted many good drivers, kept careful count of the number of laps each driver completed and made an attractive profit. Thereafter, France continued to promote the annual February beach race.

France launched his first "national" body in 1946: the National Championship Stock Car Circuit, which sponsored races all over the Southeast. After a year of operation, the N.C.S.C.C. still seemed no different from the many other regional organizations. Another effort was needed and this came in December 1947, when France and about 25 drivers and officials holed up at a bar called the Ebony Room for four days of meetings. France and his associates took Red Vogt's suggestion to call their organization the National Association of Stock Car Auto Racing and, from there, NASCAR was born with Bill France as its first president.

NASCAR sanctioned races in three divisions in its 1948 debut season: Modified (heavily modified cars), Roadsters (low-slung cars) and Strictly Stock (showroom-quality models). The Strictly Stock division was a break with racing's heritage, as racing brand new cars was unheard of. Although France believed the appeal of the Strictly Stock division was the key to NASCAR's future, the post-war shortage of new cars forced France to market the Modified as NASCAR's most prominent division. NASCAR's first race, a Modified event held on February 15, 1948 at Daytona Beach, featured nearly 50 drivers and was

Red Brings Home The Green!

In 1948, Robert "Red" Byron won the first official NASCAR race. In 1949, he went on to win two Strictly Stock races, becoming the first winner of what would later be known as the Winston Cup. His winnings: $5,800.

won by Red Byron. After 52 races held from Florida to Pennsylvania, NASCAR's debut season was celebrated as a success.

Pedal To The Metal: The 1950s & 1960s

Beginning in the 1950s, NASCAR racing began to change in several ways. First, NASCAR enjoyed tremendous growth, sanctioning races before thousands of fans on tracks all over the country. The growing popularity of auto racing even led NASCAR to introduce many new series, though some did not last long.

Another sign of the popularity of NASCAR racing was the paving and expansion of racetracks. The first asphalt track was built in Darlington, South Carolina in 1950 and its first race, billed as the Southern 500, was a spectacular affair witnessed by about 20,000 spectators. By 1969, all but 5 of 54 stock car races were held on asphalt tracks.

Car owner Carl Kiekaefer is largely credited with introducing innovations in the mid-1950s that are now familiar parts of the NASCAR scene. These included his placing of sponsors on cars, transporting race cars on trucks, maintaining a stable of multiple cars and drilling a team of professional pit men dressed in matching uniforms.

In 1951, the era of automobile-industry sponsorship began when Marshall Teague, who won the opening race of the season in a Hudson Hornet, contracted with an appreciative Hudson for cars and parts. Later that year, Bill France opened the door to a relationship between NASCAR and automobile manufacturers by staging a race in Detroit on the city's 250th anniversary celebration. Soon, car manufacturers were waging their corporate battles through NASCAR racers. The manufacturers pushed the envelope in their car designs, which caused friction with NASCAR officials. By the late 1960s, innovations such as rear wings, larger engines and sleeker designs had pushed cars to over 200 miles an hour, speeds which NASCAR officials thought were dangerous. On the other hand, innovations such as shoulder harnesses, new fuel cells, roll cages, improved helmets and tire liners helped improve safety.

Straightaway: The 1970s & 1980s

In 1972, Bill France retired as NASCAR President in favor of his son, Bill Jr. The younger France proved to be as able as his father and led NASCAR into an exciting new age.

Driver safety was still an issue for NASCAR officials, who instituted several rules in an effort to curb dangerous racing speeds. Carburetor restrictor plates appeared in 1970 and the following year saw a limit on engine sizes. Other regulations in the 1980s that changed the face of NASCAR racing included the introduction of cars with power steering, reduced wheelbase requirements and smaller carburetors.

Perhaps the biggest single change in NASCAR's fortunes came when R.J. Reynolds stepped in as a major sponsor of the sport in the early 1970s. This marked the first major NASCAR sponsorship from a com-

An Increase In Precision And Purses

The 1950s and 1960s marked the transition of NASCAR into the sport we're familiar with today. With improvements in car design and increases in speed, drivers were forced to adjust their skills to stay at the top of the sport. It was also at this time that the increased fame of the sport brought in higher revenues, the pinnacle of which was when Fred Lorenzen became the first driver to hit six figures in 1963.

pany that did not produce automobile products and soon other companies followed suit. New sponsorships translated into increased race purses. Most importantly, the R.J. Reynolds contract came with a television package which provided for taped national broadcasts of NASCAR races. As corporations took greater interest in NASCAR, more and more of the races took corporate names: the Southern 500 became the Heinz 500, Charlotte's World 600 became the Coca-Cola 600 and so forth.

Television was crucial to the expansion of racing's popularity through the 1970s and 1980s. The age of taped broadcasts and live "final lap" break-away coverage officially ended with the first live broadcast of a major NASCAR event from start to finish – the 1979 Daytona 500. Within a few years, cable and network television combined to carry every major NASCAR race, completing NASCAR's transition from a regional draw to a national sport.

One result of the media spotlight was a shift in attention from the cars to the drivers. Ultimately, the success of NASCAR in the 1970s and 1980s resulted in a shift in the public persona of the drivers. Gone were the bootleggers and rough riders of the old days; modern NASCAR drivers were professional corporate men, media savvy and endorsement friendly, who actively cultivated relationships with their legions of devoted fans.

NASCAR® The 1990s

Whatever racing fans' opinions about the growing corporate presence in NASCAR racing, it certainly helped spur the tremendous popularity of the sport in the 1990s. NASCAR's popularity reached all-time highs, with new tracks built all over the United States and even exhibition races held in Japan. NASCAR collectibles, particularly die-cast models, were heavily marketed during the 1990s, and the Craftsman Truck Series was formed in response to the growing popularity of those vehicles on American roads. Other innovations included the prevalence of multi-car teams, the use of laptops in the pits and increased specialization of crew members.

2000 & Beyond

With multi-million dollar race purses and official merchandise sales in excess of one billion dollars a year, NASCAR racing seems poised for even greater heights. How will advancing technology affect NASCAR racing? What other countries will jump on the NASCAR bandwagon? Will any more new series be started? The answers to these questions will be part of the exciting world of NASCAR racing in the new millennium!

NASCAR®: A Nationwide Phenomenon

Who would have guessed it? Back in the 1940s, when a bunch of moonshine runners met on weekends to race against each other, who would have guessed that in less than three generations their illicit activities would have evolved into a family sport loved throughout the country? Since NASCAR ran its first race in 1949, it has evolved from a local Southern phenomenon to a nationwide sport that's even starting to develop an international fan base.

NASCAR® On The Air

Much of the growth in NASCAR's popularity can be attributed to its strong television presence. For its first several decades, NASCAR could never be seen on television. Network executives considered stock car racing little more than a weekend diversion, certainly not a sport with a national fan base worthy of air time alongside football and basketball.

In those early days, what television coverage racing did receive was given little respect. Benny Parsons, the 1973 Winston Cup champion who now broadcasts for ESPN, put it most succinctly: "[NASCAR racing] was primarily on [ABC's] *Wide World of Sports* stuck between arm wrestling and cliff diving."

The first national television coverage of a NASCAR race came in 1960, when CBS showed a two-hour tape of the qualifying races for the Daytona 500. The next year, ABC included scenes from the Firecracker 250 in a *Wide World of Sports* broadcast. These occasional bits and pieces of NASCAR races were all television had to offer fans until the 1979 Daytona 500, when CBS gambled that the race, all five hours of it, would grab ratings from around the country.

That Daytona 500 was a ratings success and CBS has broadcast the race every year since. Yet NASCAR still had a very limited presence on the air for the next several years, with the networks broadcasting races or racing news very sporadically. The first regularly televised racing segments came in 1981, when cable station TBS debuted its show *MotorWeek Illustrated.* It aired for five seasons and gave racing fans information and updates on what was happening in the sport.

In 1983, the first in-car cameras were introduced, fans were given an insider's view of the action that they didn't previously have. In 1988, the cameras were refined, with heavy, bulky cameras replaced by tiny, modern "lipstick cameras" that could be mounted anywhere in a car, giving views from all different angles.

Despite these technological advances, racing still had a very limited presence on television until the advent of ESPN. The young network, devoted to sports programming, bought the broadcast rights to many races, since the rights sold very cheaply at the time. ESPN went on to become the primary source of racing broadcasts until 1991, when cable's country-music-themed The Nashville Network (TNN), realizing that many of its viewers were already race fans, bought the rights to several Winston Cup races and almost all of the Busch races that season.

TNN's gamble paid off, both in increased ratings and increased advertising revenues. The races even attracted new sponsors who had not previously bought airtime on TNN.

Around The USA With NASCAR®

In NASCAR's Winston and Busch series, most of the racetracks are concentrated in the Southeast, but not all of them. In fact, for fans who wish to see a NASCAR race, racetracks can be found as far north as New Hampshire and as far west as California. However, depending on where a fan lives, going to see a Winston Cup or Busch race might still necessitate a drive of several hundred miles.

For fans who wish to stay closer to home, there are many other race series in NASCAR. The Winston, Busch and Craftsman Truck series are the best known, but there are also the Busch North Series covering the New England states, the Raybestos Brakes Series running in the Pacific Northwest and the Featherlite Southwest Series, which of course runs in the Southwest. NASCAR fans in the heartland are especially lucky – they have two NASCAR series in their part of the country: the REMAX Challenge Series and the O'Reilly All-Star Series (also known as the Busch All-Star Series), which is notable for being the last dirt-track series in NASCAR. Other NASCAR series include the Winston West Series, the Slim Jim All Pro, the Featherlite Modified, the Goody's Dash Series and the Weekly Racing Series.

NASCAR® Cuisine

If you take your next family vacation in Orlando, Myrtle Beach, Nashville, Las Vegas or the Smoky Mountains, you'll want to stop in for dinner at the NASCAR® Cafe, the only chain of restaurants licensed by NASCAR. The first NASCAR® Cafe opened in Nashville and was an instant success. The 40,000-square-foot building is a combination restaurant, NASCAR museum and mini-game park. Ten people at a time can enjoy the racing simulator ride, which replicates the experience of driving (and crashing!) in a stock car race and there are racing-simulation video games such as *Daytona USA*.

The menu selections are named after NASCAR themes, with "Qualifying Lap" describing the appetizers menu, "Liquid Fuel" heading the beverage menu and "Sweet Success" listing all of the desserts. The restaurants do a lot of business and though visitors might have to wait for a table, they can pass the time by looking at all the NASCAR memorabilia (up to and including actual winning race cars!), playing the video games or watching the racing highlights on any of the big screen television sets. Sometimes, NASCAR drivers will even make an appearance, but whether they do or not, a trip to the NASCAR® Cafe is sure to be a memorable experience for any race fan!

A Day In The Park With NASCAR®

Just outside the entrance to Daytona International Speedway is DAYTONA USA, the first NASCAR theme park. In addition to thrill rides, the park features various NASCAR exhibits including the winning car of the most recent Daytona 500. The park is open from 9 a.m. to 7 p.m. every day except Christmas, with extended hours during race periods. Adult admission is $16, plus an additional charge for those wishing to take a Speedway Tour. Admission for seniors over 60 is $14 dollars, children between the ages of 6 and $12 pay $11 to get in and children under 6 get in free when accompanied by a paying adult. For more information, call DAYTONA USA at (904) 947-6800.

NASCAR® On The Air: Part II

Once upon a time, NASCAR had hardly any television presence at all, but now it's become so popular that, in addition to the televised races, NASCAR even has its own cartoon show! The Fox Kids network started airing the *NASCAR® Racers* cartoon series in February of 2000. The show is set in the future and shows the trials and tribulations of the four Team Fastex drivers as they hammer out their own personal problems while competing against the evil racers on their arch-rival team, Team Rexton.

The NASCAR racers in the cartoon have cars that would be the envy of any real NASCAR racer. Aerodynamic panels increase control of the car and let it go airborne for hundreds of feet at a time, while morphing tires change to meet the track or weather conditions, and turbojet and rocket boosters give an added bit of speed whenever necessary. There's even an eject button to get drivers out of their cars before they crash! It may be awhile before NASCAR fans can see such technological marvels in real life, but those who don't have the patience to wait can watch *NASCAR® Racers* on Saturday mornings.

NASCAR® Racers

Now you can experience all of the action that you see on Fox Kids' popular cartoon, *NASCAR® Racers* – right in your own living room! Hasbro Interactive and Saban Entertainment are working together to create an interactive game for the Sony PlayStation and the PC based on the cartoon. The games will feature the main characters from the cartoon, as well as high-tech race cars that can be customized to fit each player's preferences.

Driver Biographies

Despite what some people might think, driving in a NASCAR race is far different from driving on the highway. Forget traveling at a sedate 65 miles an hour while taking care to stay at least three car lengths behind the car in front of you: NASCAR drivers have excellent reflexes that allow them to pilot cars at speeds of well over 100 miles an hour while mere inches away from other cars; all without getting into an accident. Drivers need great physical endurance to stay focused on a race while spending several hours in a car with internal temperatures soaring over 120 degrees.

When not driving in a race, practicing for a race, qualifying for a race or working out to get in condition for a race, drivers spend much of their time making personal appearances for their sponsors, signing autographs and meeting with their fans. In fact, the few hours a week drivers actually spend racing only makes up a very minor part of their work schedule.

Unlike some other professional athletes, NASCAR drivers make themselves readily available to their fans, posing for pictures and sometimes giving autographs. In fact, many NASCAR drivers' fan club sites advertise that fans may send in items to be autographed.

The following is a look at a few of the men who have followed their dreams to become professional race car drivers. Read on to learn their struggles and successes as they worked to become members of the elite stock car racing division in the United States, the Winston Cup.

Jeff Burton

Jeff Burton was born on June 29, 1967, in South Boston, Virginia. His interest in racing dates back to when he was 5 years old and watched his older brother, future Winston Cup driver Ward Burton, race go-karts. Burton himself started racing go-karts at the age of 8 and later moved on to racing in the Late Model division.

As a teenager attending Halifax County High School, Burton proved himself to be a gifted athlete, standing out in basketball and serving as captain of the soccer team. Despite his prowess in other sports, Burton chose to continue racing and in 1986 he became the youngest driver in NASCAR history to win a Late Model Stock Car race. 1989 saw his first full season in the NASCAR Busch Series and he won his first Grand National race in 1990. By 1993, Burton moved up to the Winston Cup Series, qualifying sixth for his first start at the New Hampshire International Speedway. This caught the attention of the Stavola brothers, who added him to their Winston Cup racing team the following year. In 1994, he made headlines when he beat out many other drivers (including his brother Ward) for the Winston Cup Rookie Of The Year. Since then, Burton has continued to enjoy a stellar career. In 1999, he celebrated six trips to Victory Lane and took home two Winston No Bull million-dollar bonuses.

Jeff Burton Fan Club

235-10 Rolling Hills Road
Mooresville, NC 28117

Individual membership – $10.00
Family membership – $12.00

Burton married his wife, Kim, in 1992 and in 1995 their daughter Kimberle "Paige" was born. In his spare time, Burton enjoys watching the Duke University basketball team and considers Duke coach Mike Krzyzewski his favorite sports personality. Burton and his family live in Cornelius, North Carolina.

Dale Earnhardt®

Born Ralph Dale Earnhardt on April 29, 1951 in Kannapolis, North Carolina, Earnhardt spent much spare time with his dad, Ralph, in his racing shop behind the house. Eventually, his responsibilities around the shop increased and Earnhardt's dream of becoming a race car driver flourished.

Racing cars soon became an obsession, causing Earnhardt to quit school when he was 16 and by the time he was 18, he was racing full-time. After racing the Sportsman circuit for a time, Earnhardt started his first Winston Cup race in 1975.

Earnhardt made a name for himself in his 1979 rookie season, as he placed in thc top five 11 times, finished 7th in the final point standings and easily won the Winston Cup Rookie Of The Year award. In 1980, he won his first Winston Cup Championship, marking the first time in NASCAR history that a driver won Rookie Of The Year and the Winston Cup Championship in consecutive years.

Earnhardt has since won Winston Cup Championships six more times. Only one more NASCAR challenge remains for Earnhardt – the quest for a record-breaking eighth Winston Cup.

Together Earnhardt and his wife Teresa spearhead Dale Earnhardt, Inc. (DEI), a multi-million dollar company which owns two Winston Cup racing teams, a Busch Series team and a Chevrolet dealership. The couple has four children, three of whom, Kerry, Kelly and Dale Jr., have tried their hand at racing, although sons Kerry and Dale Jr. are the only ones currently active.

Club E

1480 S. Hohokam Drive
Tempe, AZ 85281

1-888-33-CLUB-E or
www.earnhardtfan.com

Individual membership –
$19.99 + $5.50 S&H

Dale Earnhardt Jr.

Living up to a legend is never easy, but so far Dale Earnhardt Jr. has more than held his own as he's followed in his famous father's footsteps. The senior Earnhardt's youngest son was born on October 10, 1974 and was raised in Concord, North Carolina. His professional driving career began at age 17, running street stock races at Concord Speedway. Only two seasons later, his driving skills sharpened enough for him to join NASCAR's Late Model Stock Division and he later moved to the Busch Series.

In his first Busch event, Earnhardt Jr. started in the 7th place position and finished 13th, a respectable showing for a beginner. He won his first Busch race at the Texas Motor Speedway in 1998 and went on to occupy the number-one position in the point standings for two years in a row. He also holds the single-season record for monetary winnings on the Busch circuit, with $1,680,598.

His first Winston Cup race was less encouraging. Earnhardt Jr. qualified to start in 8th place for the 1999 Coca-Cola 600, but during the race he had trouble finding his pit during his first stop, costing him several seconds. Despite this inauspicious beginning, Earnhardt Jr. went on to run five races that year and in the Winston Cup final point standings he ranked number 48 out of 69. Seven races into the 2000 season he had his first Winston Cup win, after only his 12th start.

Earnhardt Jr., who is single, lives in Mooresville, North Carolina, where he enjoys spending time with his family, working on computers and all types of music.

Club E Jr.

1480 S. Hohokam Drive
Tempe, AZ 85281

1-877-CLUB-E-JR or
www.dalejr.com

Individual membership – $19.99 + $5.50 S&H

Jeff Gordon®

Jeff Gordon was born on August 4, 1971 in Vallejo, California. His parents divorced when he was young and his mother later married John Bickford, who encouraged Gordon's need for speed. The boy got his first taste of horsepower when Bickford introduced him to quarter midget race cars at the age of five. By 1979, he was a national champion and would eventually capture two more championships as well as four go-cart championships.

His family moved to Indiana when Gordon was a teen. At the age of 16, he earned his racing license from the United States Auto Club. He won the USAC Midget Series National Championship in 1990, followed by the USAC Silver Crown Division National Championship a year later.

In Gordon's first season of Busch racing he racked up five finishes in the top-five, including one pole. He made the jump to full-time Winston Cup racing in 1993, where he had 30 starts and was named the Winston Cup Rookie Of The Year. 1995 saw his first Winston Cup Championship, followed by a repeat performance in 1997, the same year that Gordon became the youngest driver ever to win the legendary Daytona 500. Gordon has since won a third Winston Cup Championship; taking the title in 1998.

A family man, Gordon donates much of his winnings to charities such as the Hendrick Marrow Program, an offshoot of The Marrow Foundation which seeks bone marrow matches for leukemia patients. He has been married since 1994 to Brooke Sealy, a former Miss Winston.

Jeff Gordon Fan Club

1480 S. Hohokam Drive
Tempe, AZ 85281

1-877-JEFF-GORDON or
www.jeffgordon.com

Individual membership – $19.99 + $5.50 S&H

Dale Jarrett®

Dale Jarrett, the son of former NASCAR star Ned Jarrett, was born on November 26, 1956 and raised in Conover, North Carolina. As a child, he went to the tracks to watch his father, but never considered racing as a career. At Newton-Conover High School, Jarrett was a star quarterback, shortstop and basketball player and so talented a golfer that the University of South Carolina offered him a scholarship. He turned it down and chose to take a job at Hickory Motor Speedway, which his father owned.

At the age of 20, Jarrett started working on a race car with some high school friends. After convincing his father to loan him money for an engine, Jarrett drove the car in his first race. He started 25th, finished ninth and realized that he had found his calling.

Jarrett began racing in the Limited Sportsman Division at the Hickory Motor Speedway in 1977 and moved to the Busch Series in 1982, the division's debut year. In 1984, Jarrett drove in his first Winston Cup race and began racing in the series full-time three years later. Also in 1997, Jarrett won the True Value Man Of The Year award from which he donated his prize money to Brenner Children's Hospital, one of the many charities with which he is involved. Jarrett enjoyed a stellar year in 1999, at the end of which he was named Winston Cup Champion.

Dale Jarrett and his wife, Kelley, have four children and the family currently lives in Hickory, North Carolina. In his spare time, Jarrett enjoys playing golf and, of course, watching sports.

Dale Jarrett Fan Club

1480 S. Hohokam Drive
Tempe, AZ 85281

1-888-DALE-JARRETT or
www.dalejarrett.com

Individual membership – $19.99
+ $5.50 S&H

Bobby Labonte™

Bobby Labonte was born in Corpus Christi, Texas, on May 8, 1964. His interest in racing stems from watching his older brother, two-time Winston Cup Champion Terry Labonte. Labonte started driving quarter midgets in 1969 when he was just 5 years old, go-karts in 1978 and in 1979, the Labonte family moved to North Carolina where Labonte eventually became a crew member for Hagan Racing.

Labonte started driving Late Model Stocks soon after, moving on to win the championship in 1987. He moved to the Busch Series in 1990 and was honored with the series' Most Popular Driver award that same year. His first Winston Cup start came in 1991, the same year he was named the BGN National Champion. He lost the 1992 championship by only three points and the following year he started concentrating full-time on the Winston Cup circuit.

Joe Gibbs Racing hired Labonte to replace Dale Jarrett in 1995. Labonte proved himself to be an excellent addition to the team when he went on to win three races that season, finishing 10th in the standings. Since then, Labonte has enjoyed continued success, winning at least one race each season.

When he's not driving real cars, Labonte enjoys operating remote-controlled ones and his other hobbies include flying and watching the Dallas Cowboys. He and his wife Donna have two children, Tyler and Madison, and the family currently lives in Trinity, North Carolina.

Bobby Labonte Fan Club

1480 S. Hohokam Drive
Tempe, AZ 85281

1-877-4-BOBBY-L or
www.bobbylabontefan.com

Individual membership – $19.99 + $5.50 S&H

Mark Martin®

Mark Martin was born in Batesville, Arkansas on January 9, 1959. He started driving cars thanks to some unusual encouragement from his father, who, while driving over the gravel roads of their hometown, would sit Martin in his lap and let him take the wheel. Though terrified at first, Martin soon grew accustomed to piloting the car through town at speeds in excess of 80 miles per hour and came to love the sensation of speed.

In the 1970s, Martin raced with the American Speed Association, where he became a four-time champion. In 1981, he moved to the Winston Cup Series where he made a name for himself by winning two poles in five races. In 1982, he was the runner-up to Geoff Bodine for the Rookie Of The Year award.

For the past eleven seasons, Martin has finished in the top six in the Winston Cup final point standings and many people consider him to be the finest Winston Cup driver who has yet to win a championship. In addition to his Winston Cup success for the Roush Racing Team, Martin became the winningest driver in Busch Grand National history in 1998, when his 32nd victory broke Jack Ingram's previous record of 31 wins. Additionally, Martin has also garnered four IROC Championships through the years, a sport in which he continues to compete today.

Martin says his favorite hobbies are flying airplanes and weight training, though he also found time to co-author two books. Mark Martin and his wife, Arlene and their son, Matt, currently reside in Florida.

Mark Martin Fan Club

235-10 Rolling Hills Rd.
Mooresville, NC 28117

Individual membership – $11.00
Family membership – $15.00

Tony Stewart®

Though he may be new to the world of Winston Cup, Tony Stewart is already an old hand at racing. Born May 20, 1971 in Rushville, Indiana, Stewart got his start racing go-karts at age 8. He soon captured the 1983 International Karting Foundation Championship and the 1987 World Karting Association national titles. He followed up these successes with a 1991 Rookie Of The Year title in the United States Auto Club's Sprint Car division and the 1995 titles in the three top divisions of the USAC.

Stewart continued to work his way up through the ranks of go-karts, sprint and midget cars until 1996, when he won the Indianapolis 500 Rookie Of The Year award based on his showing during the race. 1996 was also the year that Stewart made his NASCAR debut with nine Busch Series races. He has continued to race both in Indy and in NASCAR over the years and, in 1999, Stewart became the first driver in Winston Cup history to win three races in his rookie year. Stewart was also the first rookie since 1966 to finish the season in the top five. He is also the first driver to complete both the Indianapolis 500 and the Coca-Cola 600 on the same day.

Not surprisingly, Stewart won the 1999 Rookie Of The Year award, which was soon followed by the Eastern Motorsport Press Association's prestigious Driver Of The Year award in January 2000. Stewart has homes in Indiana and North Carolina. He is still single and his hobbies include boating and playing pool.

Tony Stewart Fan Club

5671 W. 74th St.
Indianapolis, IN 46278-1755

1-800-867-6067 or
www.tonystewart.com

Individual membership – $20.00

Rusty Wallace®

Rusty Wallace, a St. Louis native, was born on August 14, 1956 and made his racing debut at 17 when he ran on the Lakehill Speedway, located near Valley Park, Missouri in 1973. Wallace was named the Central Auto Racing Association Rookie Of The Year in 1973 and he went on to win over 200 races before he joined the stock car circuit of the United States Auto Club in 1979, where he again became Rookie Of The Year. Wallace started competing in Winston Cup races part-time in 1980 and in his very first Winston Cup race he amazed fans and drivers alike by finishing in an unprecedented second place.

In 1983, Wallace was named the American Speed Association's Series Champion and the following year he began racing in the Winston Cup full-time. Wallace picked up a Winston Cup Rookie Of The Year title in 1984 and celebrated his first NASCAR win two years later at Bristol. Since then, Wallace has won at least one race every season. In 1989, he won the Winston Cup Championship and the National Motorsports Press Association named him Driver Of The Year in 1988 and yet again in 1993. 2000 has been a milestone year for the driver, who celebrated both his 500th start and his 50th victory in the Winston Cup recently.

Even when not racing, Wallace likes to keep himself busy. He has written a column for the web site, *goracing.com* and currently writes for the CNN/Sports Illustrated site. Wallace and his wife, Patti, have three children: Greg, Katie and Stephen.

Rusty Wallace Fan Club

1480 S. Hohokam Drive
Tempe, AZ 85281

1-877-RUSTY-WALLACE or
www.rustywallace.com

Individual membership – $19.99 + $5.50 S&H

Today's Top Racers

Although it may look easy, racing is a tough sport. It takes years of practice to race with such precision and speed. So while many drivers race every year, only a few are lucky enough to make it to NASCAR's toughest division – the Winston Cup. Here is a look at 1999's top 25 points winners and their Winston Cup stats.

1. Dale Jarrett®

Car Number: 88

Team: Robert Yates Racing

Sponsor: Quality Care

Years Racing: 16

2. Bobby Labonte™

Car Number: 18

Team: Joe Gibbs Racing

Sponsor: Interstate Batteries

Years Racing: 9

3. Mark Martin®

Car Number: 6

Team: Roush Racing

Sponsor: Valvoline

Years Racing: 18

4. Tony Stewart®

Car Number: 20

Team: Joe Gibbs Racing

Sponsor: Home Depot

Years Racing: 2

5. Jeff Burton

Car Number: 99

Team: Roush Racing

Sponsor: Exide Batteries

Years Racing: 8

6. Jeff Gordon®

Car Number: 24

Team: Hendrick Motorsports

Sponsor: DuPont

Years Racing: 9

7. Dale Earnhardt®

Car Number: 3

Team: Richard Childress Racing

Sponsor: GM Goodwrench

Years Racing: 26

8. Rusty Wallace®

Car Number: 2

Team: Penske South Racing

Sponsor: Miller Lite

Years Racing: 21

9. Ward Burton

Car Number: 22

Team: Bill Davis Racing

Sponsor: Caterpillar

Years Racing: 7

10. Mike Skinner

Car Number: 31

Team: Richard Childress Racing

Sponsor: Lowe's

Years Racing: 10

11. Jeremy Mayfield

Car Number: 12

Team: Penske-Kranefuss Racing

Sponsor: Mobil 1

Years Racing: 8

12. Terry Labonte

Car Number: 5

Team: Hendrick Motorsports

Sponsor: Kellogg's

Years Racing: 23

13. Bobby Hamilton

Car Number: 4

Team: Morgan-McClure Motorsports

Sponsor: Kodak Max

Years Racing: 11

14. Steve Park

Car Number: 1

Team: Dale Earnhardt Inc.

Sponsor: Pennzoil

Years Racing: 4

15. Ken Schrader

Car Number: 36
Team: MB2 Motorsports
Sponsor: M&Ms
Years Racing: 17

16. Sterling Marlin

Car Number: 40
Team: Team SABCO
Sponsor: Coors Light
Years Racing: 24

17. John Andretti

Car Number: 43
Team: Petty Enterprises
Sponsor: STP/Cheerios
Years Racing: 8

18. Wally Dallenbach Jr.

Car Number: 75
Team: Galaxy Motorsports
Sponsor: Turner Broadcasting
Years Racing: 13

19. Jimmy Spencer

Car Number: 26
Team: Travis Carter Motorsports
Sponsor: Big Kmart
Years Racing: 12

20. Bill Elliott™

Car Number: 94
Team: Bill Elliott Racing
Sponsor: McDonald's
Years Racing: 24

21. Kenny Wallace

Car Number: 55
Team: Andy Petree Racing
Sponsor: Square D
Years Racing: 10

22. Chad Little

Car Number: 97
Team: Roush Racing
Sponsor: John Deere
Years Racing: 15

23. Elliott Sadler

Car Number: 21
Team: Wood Brothers Racing
Sponsor: Citgo
Years Racing: 3

24. Kevin Lepage

Car Number: 16
Team: Roush Racing
Sponsor: Familyclick.com
Years Racing: 4

25. Kyle Petty

Car Number: 44
Team: Petty Enterprises
Sponsor: Hot Wheels
Years Racing: 22

Ones To Watch

These guys may not be among 1999's top racers, but they stand a good chance of ranking among the top racers of tomorrow!

Casey Atwood – Atwood began making a name for himself at the age of 17, when he became the youngest driver in NASCAR Busch Series history. In 1999, he topped this record, becoming the youngest driver to win a Busch race.

Dave Blaney – This accomplished open-wheel racing champion made the move to the Winston Cup Series in 1998. Since then, he has shown steady improvement as a driver including five top-5 and 12 top-10 finishes, as well as four Bud Poles in 31 races in 1999.

Ricky Craven – After recovering from injuries from the 1997 season, this former Rookie Of The Year is back and – so it seems – better than ever. Craven is known for his talent, skill and competitive edge.

Matt Kenseth – A strong contender for the 2000 Winston Cup Rookie Of The Year award, Kenseth has had four finishes in the top five this year. Often compared to Roush Racing teammate Mark Martin, this Cambridge, Wisconsin native is definitely one to keep an eye on!

Joe Nemechek – Since he joined the Winston Cup circuit full-time in 1994, "Front Row Joe" has enjoyed a solid career. Consistently ranking in the top 30 in the points standings, Nemechek celebrated his first trip to Victory Lane in 1999 at the New Hampshire Motor Speedway.

Who's Who In The Pit Crew

NASCAR drivers need an extraordinary amount of skill to win a race, but they also need a good pit crew; as the greatest driver in the world won't win a race if his crew needs five minutes every time he stops. Here are the people you'll see on a NASCAR pit crew:

The Crew Chief: The Crew Chief is like a combination football coach and pit boss. He determines who does what in the crew and often decides when the driver needs stop. Crew chiefs have to be good mechanics and will sometimes fill in for other pit members as needed.

Front Tire Changer: The front tire changer changes the left and right front tires.

Rear Tire Changer: Just like the front tire changer, only he works at the rear end of the car.

Tire Carrier: There are usually two tire carriers, one each for the front and back of the car. In addition to carrying the tires, they also help guide them onto the lugs. Sometimes the front tire carrier also has to clean the car's grille.

Jack Man: The jack man has to work faster than anyone else in the pit crew. His job is to jack the car up, as until he does his job the tire changers are unable to complete their work. The jack man raises the right side of the car first and after that is complete, he moves on to the left.

Gas Man: A gas man has to be very strong, since a full gas can can weigh up to 90 pounds and most pit stops require two cans worth of gasoline.

Gas Catch Man: While the gas man refuels the car, the gas catch man catches any fuel that overflows. To do this, he holds a special container (known as a "catch can") up to the car's gasoline overflow vent, so as to catch any gasoline flowing out from an already-full tank. Gas catch men also have to be very strong since their responsibilities sometimes include holding the second gas can on their shoulders.

Other Team Members

NASCAR rules mandate that only seven members of the pit crew can be "over the wall" at any one time. However, there are other people who perform invaluable duties for the race team, even if they aren't actually in the pits. Sometimes a crew member will stand behind the wall and use a long pole to give a driver a drink. There are also "spotters," crucial team members who sit in the control tower and spend the race in constant communication with the driver, telling him what obstacles are on the track, where the race leader is and other such information. The spotter tells the driver everything he needs to know but he can't see for himself. There are also crew members who wash the windshield, fill the gas cans and hold the pit board.

Gone In 20 Seconds

A win depends not only on the driver, but also on his pit crew. A good pit crew can make all the difference, which is why there is fierce competition among the crews. Once a year, pit crews get to confront each other in the Union 76-Rockingham Pit Crew Championship. At the championship, pit crews prove their servicing skills. In 1999, Bobby Labonte's crew won with a record time of 19.166 seconds, thus setting a new servicing standard.

Track Guide

Twenty-one different racetracks will host Winston Cup races for the 2000 season. Below is a guide containing basic facts about each one, including ticket information, the degree of banking on the corners (CB) and straightaways (SB), and, of course, the track lengths.

Atlanta Motor Speedway

P.O. Box 500, Hampton, GA 30228 • Tickets: 770-946-4211
Length: 1.54 miles • **CB:** 24 • **SB:** 5

The Atlanta Motor Speedway hosts two Winston Cup races each year. Atlanta also hosts an annual Busch series race, music festivals and other civic events.

Bristol Motor Speedway

P.O. Box 3966, Bristol, TN 37625 • Tickets: 423-764-1161
Length: 0.533 miles • **CB:** 36 • **SB:** 16

Bristol boasts the fastest and steepest racetrack on the Winston Cup circuit. Almost every spectator's seat provides an excellent view of the track, making this an especially popular venue for the fans.

California Speedway

9300 Cherry Ave., Fontana, CA 92335 • Tickets: 800-944-7223
Length: 2 miles • **CB:** 14 • **SB:** (frontstretch) 11, (backstretch) 3

California Speedway is one of NASCAR's younger venues, having opened in 1997. The Speedway hosts races and also a ""Taste of California" festival featuring foods and wines from across the state.

Darlington Raceway

P.O. Box 500, Darlington, SC 29532 • Tickets: 843-395-8499
Length: 1.366 miles • **CB:** (1-2) 25, (3-4) 23 • **SB:** 2

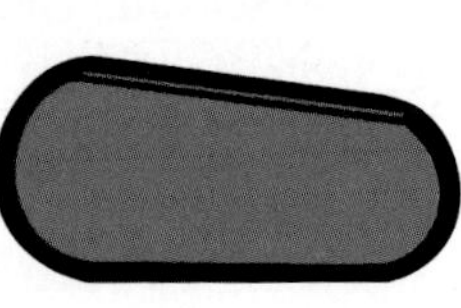

NASCAR drivers are particularly proud of wins at Darlington, the raceway many consider "Too Tough to Tame." Darlington is also home to the NMPA Stock Car Hall of Fame/Joe Weatherly Museum.

Daytona International Speedway

P.O. Box 2801, Daytona Beach, FL 32114 • Tickets: 904-253-RACE
Length: 2.5 miles • **CB:** 31 • **SB:** 6

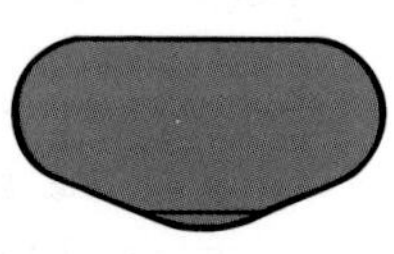

Daytona International Speedway has the Daytona USA theme-park just outside its gates where fans can enjoy the rides and also see the winning car of that year's Daytona 500 on display.

Dover Downs International Speedway

P.O. Box 843, Dover, DE 19903 • Tickets: 800-441-RACE
Length: 1 mile • **CB:** 24 • **SB:** 9

Known as "The Monster Mile," Dover Downs has hosted Winston Cup races ever since it was built in 1969. The Speedway is the largest sports facility in the Northeast.

Homestead-Miami Speedway

1 Speedway Blvd., Homestead, FL 33035
Tickets: 305-230-RACE
Length: 1.5 miles • **CB:** 6 • **SB:** 3

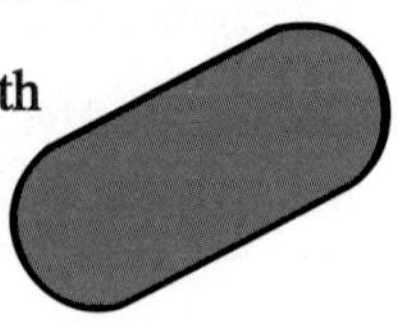

NASCAR racing came to Miami in 1995 with the opening of this speedway, which hosted the season finale of that year's Busch Series..

Indianapolis Motor Speedway

4790 W. 16th St., Indianapolis, IN 46222 • Tickets: 317-484-6700
Length: 2.5 miles • **CB:** 9 • **SB:** 0

The speedway is nicknamed "The Brickyard" after the 3.2 million bricks once used to pave the track. Though later repaved with asphalt, most of the bricks are still in place underneath; and a "yard of bricks" remains at the start/finish line.

Las Vegas Motor Speedway

7000 Las Vegas Blvd., North Las Vegas, NV 89115
Tickets: 800-644-4444
Length: 1.5 miles • **CB:** 12 • **SB:** (frontstretch) 9, (backstretch) 3

Las Vegas hosted its first NASCAR race in 1996, with the season finale of the Craftsman Truck series. Busch and Winston both race here.

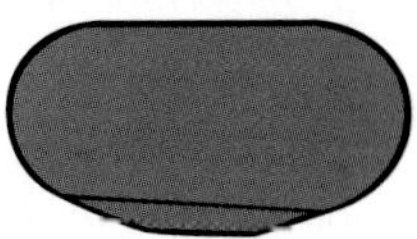

Lowe's Motor Speedway

P.O. Box 600, Concord, NC 28026 • Tickets: 800-455-FANS
Length: 1.5 miles • **CB:** 24 • **SB:** 5

This is the largest sports facility in the Southeast. The Speedway hosts three Winston Cup races each year and in 1992, it became the first superspeedway to host a race at night.

Martinsville Speedway

P.O. Box 3311, Martinsville, VA 24112 • Tickets: 540-956-3151
Length: 0.526 miles • **CB:** 12 • **SB:** 0

Martinsville Speedway predates NASCAR by two years, having opened in 1947. NASCAR has run races there since 1949, though originally on dirt tracks. This is the oldest racetrack on the circuit.

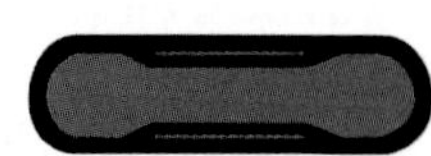

Michigan Speedway

12626 U.S. Highway 12, Brooklyn, MI 49230
Tickets: 800-354-1010
Length: 2 miles • **CB:** 18
SB: (frontstretch) 12, (backstretch) 5

Michigan Speedway opened in 1968 and held its first NASCAR race in 1969. Popular with spectators thanks to the excellent views, the track's wide racing surfaces and high banks make it one of the premier facilities in motorsports.

New Hampshire International Speedway

P.O. Box 7888, Loudon, NH 03301
Tickets: 603-783-4931
Length: 1.058 miles • **CB:** 12 • **SB:** 5

The northernmost track in NASCAR is also among the youngest. Built in 1990, the track hosts races in all of NASCAR's series as well as events for the American Motorsports Association.

North Carolina Speedway

P.O. Box 500, Rockingham, NC 28360
Tickets: 910-582-2861
Length: 1.017 miles • **CB:** (1-2) 22, (3-4) 25 • **SB:** 8

Usually referred to as Rockingham, the North Carolina Speedway was built in 1965 and its first race, the NASCAR American 500, was held on Halloween the same year.

Phoenix International Raceway

7602 S. 115th Ave., Avondale, AZ 85323
Tickets: 602-252-2227
Length: 1 mile • **CB:** (1-2) 11, (3-4) 9 • **SB:** 0

The "Desert Mile" opened in 1964 and has hosted all sorts of races, from NASCAR to Indy. The track was repaved in 1993.

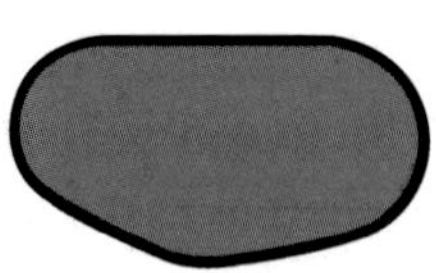

Pocono Raceway

P.O. Box 500, Long Pond, PA 18334 • Tickets: 800-RACEWAY
Length: 2.5 miles • **CB:** (1) 14, (2) 8, (3) 6 • **SB:** 0

Pocono is one of the most competitive tracks in NASCAR, with three turns that all have a different degrees of banking. The varied turns are why Pocono is often defined as the "superspeedway that drives like a road course."

Richmond International Raceway

P.O. Box 9257, Richmond, VA 23222 • Tickets: 804-345-7223
Length: 0.75 miles • **CB:** 14
SB: (frontstretch) 8, (backstretch) 2

Lee Petty won the first Winston Cup race held here back in 1953. The facility was built on the site of a half-mile dirt track that hosted races in the 1940s.

Sears Point Raceway

Highways 37 & 121, Sonoma, CA 95476 Tickets: 800-870-7223
Length: 1.95 miles • 11 turns in course

One of only two road courses on the Winston Cup circuit, Sears Point was built in 1968 and has hosted Winston Cup races since 1989.

Talladega Superspeedway

P.O. Box 777, Talladega, AL 35161 • Tickets: 256-362-RACE
Length: 2.66 miles • **CB:** 33 • **SB:** 18 (through the tri-oval)

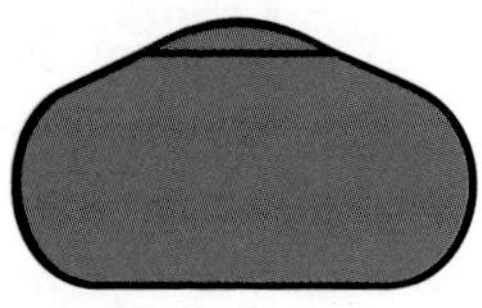

Opened in 1969, Talladega is known as the fastest course on the circuit. The Motorsports Hall of Fame and Museum is adjacent to the track.

Texas Motor Speedway

P.O Box 500 Fort Worth, TX 76101 • Tickets: 817-215-8500
Length: 1.5 miles • **CB:** 24 • **SB:** 5

This is the second-largest sports facility in the nation and the third-largest in the world. It has over 150,000 seats and a grandstand nearly two-thirds of a mile long. Winston, Busch and Craftsman Truck races are held here.

Watkins Glen International

P.O. Box 500 Watkins Glen, NY 14891 Tickets: • 607-535-2481
Length: 2.45 miles • **CB:** N/A • **SB:** N/A

Watkins Glen opened in 1948 and is one of two road courses on the circuit. Watkins Glen, with its seven right-hand turns, is considered one of the best spectator tracks. NASCAR held its first race here in 1957.

Busch Series Tracks

Races in the Busch Series are held anywhere from the famous superspeedways to small local tracks. Even if you're not lucky enough to live close to tracks like Daytona or Talladega, chances are you live within a couple of hours of a track that does host NASCAR events. Check *www.NASCAR.com* for this season's full racing schedule to see who's racing near you!

GREAT MOMENTS IN RACING

The following is a look at some of the greatest action in the history of motorsports. How many of these racing milestones did you witness?

• Though the legendary Indianapolis Motor Speedway opened to the public in 1909, the track did not host a Winston Cup event until 1994. The first race for the series, dubbed the Brickyard 400, was won by driver **Jeff Gordon**.

• In June of 1949, NASCAR's first Strictly Stock Series race was held in Charlotte, North Carolina. During the 107th lap of the race, **Lee Petty**, driving a '46 Buick, rolled his car several times and became the first driver to crash his car during a NASCAR race.

• In 1949, after dueling with fellow driver **Fonty Flock** for the lead, **Robert "Red" Byron** won the first season championship.

• In 1954, **Tim Flock** brought about a great change to the racing circuit when he established radio communications between himself and his pit crew.

• In 1955, **Fonty** and **Tim Flock** became the first brothers to both finish in the top ten points in Winston Cup history. Forty years later, history repeated itself when brothers **Bobby** and **Terry Labonte** both finished in the top ten in the Winston Cup point standings.

• In 1957, Buck Baker became the first driver to win consecutive NASCAR Winston Cup titles. At the same time he also recorded another Winston Cup record when he finished with 35 consecutive top tens.

• Lee Petty made history in 1959 when he won the first-ever Daytona 500. Adding to the excitement of this new race was a photo-finish ending between Johnny Beauchamp and Petty. In fact, Beauchamp was declared the winner until NASCAR President Bill France took a closer look at the photos and, three days later, reversed the ruling.

A "Beary" Close Call

Cale Yarborough has had many narrow brushes with death, not all of which have occurred on the track. After mentioning that he'd like to have a pet bear, some of his crew trapped a bear for him. Yarborough then flew his plane to pick up the bear, who was tied tight with plastic rope. Unfortunately, the bear gnawed through the ropes in mid-flight and almost got loose. Luckily, though, Yarborough managed to land in time to transport the bear safely to a cage.

• The second Daytona 500 proved just as exciting as the first when driver Tommy Irwin landed in Lake Lloyd after a spinout during the race.

• In 1965, Ned Jarrett won the Southern 500 by the largest margin of victory in Winston Cup history. Jarrett pulled into Victory Lane 19.25 miles, or 14 laps, ahead of his fellow drivers.

• The record for the largest number of races won in a single season is 27 and is held by Richard Petty, who reached this milestone in 1967.

• The Indianapolis 500 and the Daytona 500 are two legendary races with some of the highest spectator turnouts ever. The only two drivers to win both events are A.J. Foyt and Mario Andretti, both of whom are just as legendary as the races themselves.

• Prior to winning the Winston Cup Championship in 1970, **Bobby Isaac's** greatest accomplishment was setting the Winston Cup record for 20 poles in the 1969 season.

• At Talladega Superspeedway, **Buddy Baker** became the first driver to break the 200 mph barrier during a race.

• **David Pearson's** Winston Cup wins are second only to **Richard Petty's,** even though Pearson only started in half as many races as Petty. A friendly rivalry between the two developed throughout the years and eventually came to a head at the 1974 Firecracker 400, when Pearson and Petty vied for the lead. As they both approached the white flag, Pearson slowed and let Petty pass. Then, on the final turn, Pearson (who had briefly flicked off his ignition) refired and sailed past Petty to victory.

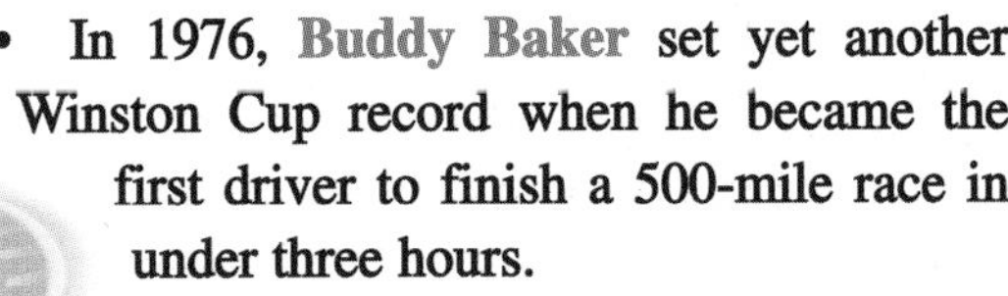

• In 1976, **Buddy Baker** set yet another Winston Cup record when he became the first driver to finish a 500-mile race in under three hours.

• The only driver to ever have won both of the famed Daytona races, the Daytona 500 and the Daytona ARCA 200, is **Benny Parsons.**

• **Darrell Waltrip** continuously pleases race fans with his wit and charm, as well as his great racing tactics. In a five year span during the 1980s, Waltrip claimed 40 victories and three Winston Cup Championships.

• The 1979 Daytona 500 was an exciting event for fans all around the country as it was the first 500-mile Winston Cup race to be televised from flag to flag.

Here's To You . . . Shawna Robinson

Shawna Robinson was 19 when she first raced in Atlanta in the Great American Truck Racing Series (GATR). The same year (1984), she became the first woman to ever win a superspeedway event in motorsports and claimed rookie honors in GATR. Before she retired from her career in the series in 1987, she had claimed four victories and placed third in points standings for two consecutive years.

• In 1979, "The Intimidator," **Dale Earnhardt,** was named Rookie of the Year. In 1980, he followed up the accomplishment by winning the title of Winston Cup Champion, thus becoming the first driver to win the two in consecutive years.

• **Geoff Bodine** changed NASCAR forever in 1981 when he introduced power steering to Winston Cup.

• In 1985, **Bill Elliott** fans had much to gloat about as "Awesome Bill from Dawsonville" won 11 superspeedway races, setting a Winston Cup record. Elliott also became the first driver to win the Winston Million by winning the Daytona 500, the Southern 500 and the Winston 500 that year; and though he lost the Winston Cup title to **Darrell Waltrip,** he earned himself the nickname "Million Dollar Bill."

• At just 22 years of age, **Bobby Hillin** became the youngest driver to win a Winston Cup race when he captured the checkered flag at Talladega in 1986. In contrast, **Harry Gant** became the oldest driver to reach victory lane when he won in 1992 at age 52.

• In 1987, **Bill Elliott** broke the record for the fastest lap ever at the Daytona International Speedway. Later that year, he trumped himself by setting the record for the fastest pole ever when he was clocked at 212.809 miles per hour at the Talladega Superspeedway.

• The 1988 Daytona 500 provided yet another spectacular finish when **Bobby Allison** and his son **Davey** competed against each other for the victory. It was a close finish, but experience won out as Bobby and Davey Allison became the only father and son to finish first and second, respectively.

• NASCAR has featured several female drivers throughout its history. One of these notable female racers, **Pattie Moise,** established the women's closed-circuit world speed record in 1990 with a 217 miles per hour lap recorded at Talladega.

Who's That Lady?

Racing, it seems, is in Geoff Bodine's blood. As a young boy growing up in New York, where his parents owned the Chemung Speedrome, he attended races on weekends. Though Bodine obviously had talent behind the wheel, his parents preferred that he work on the track rather than race on it. Looking for a way to satisfy his desire to race, the 16-year-old Bodine put on a wig and raced in an all-female Powder Puff Derby. His parents, amused by his stunt, thereafter allowed him to pursue his dreams.

• In 1992, **Dale Jarrett** won his first Winston Cup race after beating **Davey Allison** by just eight inches in Michigan, making for one of the most exciting finishes since **Richard Petty** and **David Pearson** crashed at Daytona in the final lap of the 1976 race.

• 1992 brought race fans yet another exciting rivalry when **Alan Kulwicki** and **Bill Elliott** competed for the Winston Cup title. Kulwicki won the title with the narrowest margin in NASCAR history, with only a 10-point victory over Elliott.

• History was made at the Daytona International Speedway in 1994 when **Loy Allen Jr.** not only became the first rookie to win the pole for the Daytona 500, but also to win the pole for the Daytona ARCA 500, thus becoming the only driver to have won both poles during the Speedweeks Festival.

• In 1997, **Jeff Gordon** won the Southern 500, known as "The Granddaddy of Them All," for the third year in a row.

• In 1998 at the Brickyard 400, driver **Ernie Irvan** broke the pole record that he had set the previous year. In 1997, while driving a Ford, Irvan won the Bud Pole with a record speed of 177.736 miles per hour. Then, in 1998, Irvan broke his own record with a speed of 179.394 miles-per-hour while driving a Pontiac.

• **Terry Labonte** and **Joe Nemechek** thrilled spectators at the Talladega Superspeedway with a photo finish in the 1999 Touchstone Energy 300. Labonte edged out Nemechek by a race record of two-thousandths of a second to take the victory.

• With a win in the 2000 Die Hard 500 race, **Dale Earnhardt** became the first driver to win three consecutive NASCAR Winston Cup Series races at Talladega since Buddy Baker.

Calling All Units

On his 16th birthday, Winston Cup team owner Robert Yates managed to persuade Charlotte police to let him take the driving test without first getting a permit. He passed the test and the following day he received the first of his many speeding tickets. He was so notorious for his high speed driving that the police had a special patrol car that followed Yates home from school!

Great Racers In NASCAR® History

Since NASCAR was founded in 1948, hundreds of men and women have sought success as professional race car drivers. However, when we think back on the past 52 years, there are some names which are sure to pop out in everyone's minds. These are the men who have pushed the envelope and distinguished themselves as true legends of the sport. In addition to the drivers featured in this book, this section highlights drivers who have made their mark on the sport, whether it be on the race track or off. From the earliest days of auto racing to the present, these notable men have broken records, made headlines, and helped to change the sport of NASCAR forever.

NOTE: Statistics are through the end of the 1999 race season.

Bobby Allison

Hometown: Hueytown, AL
Birthdate: 12/3/37
Years Raced: 25
Starts: 718
Wins: 85
Pole Positions: 59
Retired: 1988

Buck Baker

Hometown: Charlotte, NC
Birthdate: 3/4/19
Years Raced: 26
Starts: 636
Wins: 46
Pole Positions: 44
Retired: 1976

Buddy Baker

Hometown: Charlotte, NC
Birthdate: 1/25/41
Years Raced: 34
Starts: 699
Wins: 19
Pole Positions: 40
Retired: 1994

Ralph Earnhardt

Hometown: Kannapolis, NC
Birthdate: 2/29/28
Years Raced: 6
Starts: 51
Wins: 0
Pole Positions: 1
Retired: 1964
Deceased: 9/26/73

Neil Bonnett

Hometown: Bessemer, AL
Birthdate: 7/30/46
Years Raced: 18
Starts: 363
Wins: 18
Pole Positions: 20
Deceased: 2/11/94

Bill Elliott

© CORBIS

Hometown: Dawsonville, GA
Birthdate: 10/8/55
Years Raced: 25
Starts: 596
Wins: 40
Pole Positions: 49
Active Driver

Tim Flock

© CORBIS

Hometown: Ft. Payne, AL
Birthdate: 5/11/24
Years Raced: 13
Starts: 187
Wins: 39
Pole Positions: 39
Retired: 1961

Ned Jarrett

© DAYTONA RACING ARCHIVES

Hometown: Newton, NC
Birthdate: 10/12/32
Years Raced: 13
Starts: 352
Wins: 50
Pole Positions: 35
Retired: 1966

A.J. Foyt

© CORBIS

Hometown: Houston, TX
Birthdate: 1/16/35
Years Raced: 31
Starts: 128
Wins: 7
Pole Positions: 10
Retired: 1994

Junior Johnson

© DAYTONA RACING ARCHIVES

Hometown: Ronda, NC
Birthdate: 6/28/31
Years Raced: 14
Starts: 313
Wins: 50
Pole Positions: 47
Retired: 1966

Alan Kulwicki

© DAYTONA RACING ARCHIVES

Hometown: Greenfield, WI
Birthdate: 12/14/54
Years Raced: 9
Starts: 207
Wins: 5
Pole Positions: 24
Deceased: 4/1/93

David Pearson

Hometown: Spartanburg, SC
Birthdate: 12/22/34
Years Raced: 27
Starts: 574
Wins: 105
Pole Positions: 113
Retired: 1986

Benny Parsons

Hometown: Detroit, MI
Birthdate: 7/12/41
Years Raced: 21
Starts: 526
Wins: 21
Pole Positions: 20
Retired: 1988

Lee Petty

Hometown: Level Cross, NC
Birthdate: 3/14/14
Years Raced: 16
Starts: 427
Wins: 54
Pole Positions: 18
Retired: 1964
Deceased: 4/5/00

Richard Petty

Hometown: Level Cross, NC
Birthdate: 7/2/37
Years Raced: 35
Starts: 1184
Wins: 200
Pole Positions: 126
Retired: 1992

Ricky Rudd

© ISAAC HERNANDEZ/MERCURY PRESS

Hometown: Chesapeake, VA
Birthdate: 9/12/56
Years Raced: 26
Starts: 594
Wins: 19
Pole Positions: 23
Active Driver

Fireball Roberts

Hometown: Daytona Beach, FL
Birthdate: 1/20/29
Years Raced: 15
Starts: 206
Wins: 33
Pole Positions: 35
Deceased: 7/2/64

Darrell Waltrip

© MERCURY PRESS

Hometown: Franklin, TN
Birthdate: 2/5/47
Years Raced: 29
Starts: 720
Wins: 84
Pole Positions: 59
Active Driver – Retiring after 2000 season

Joe Weatherly

Hometown: Norfolk, VA
Birthdate: 5/29/22
Years Raced: 12
Starts: 230
Wins: 25
Pole Positions: 19
Deceased: 1/19/64

Cale Yarborough

Hometown: Timmonsville, SC
Birthdate: 3/27/39
Years Raced: 31
Starts: 559
Wins: 83
Pole Positions: 70
Retired: 1988

That's Racin'!

Race drivers are known for being extremely loyal to their sport and Ernie Irvan is no exception. During a 1994 race at the Michigan International Speedway, Irvan suffered life threatening injuries and was given only a 10 percent chance of survival. Motivated by his desire to continue racing, Irvan survived and returned a year later ready to race.

How The Race Is Run

Every sport has its own set of rules, and most of them are pretty consistent from year to year. NASCAR, however, is different, as the rules can change not only from season to season, but from race to race. Why? NASCAR officials want to make sure the playing field is as level as possible. That's why you won't see cars in NASCAR races powered by jet engines, or shaped like aerodynamic Formula One cars – because the rules don't allow it.

Change Is Good

Of course, jet engines or Formula One bodies were never allowed in NASCAR in the first place. So you may wonder how legal engines or bodies can be affected by changing rules. One famous example came during the 1998 season. Three types of cars were raced in the Winston Cup that year – the Chevrolet Monte Carlo, the Pontiac Grand Prix and the Ford Taurus. The Taurus that year was a new model, and it did very well – so well that in one race, 13 of the top 14 finishers were Ford Tauruses. Obviously the Taurus had some aerodynamic advantages over the other cars, so NASCAR changed the rules and required teams of drivers who were racing Tauruses to lower the rear spoilers by a quarter of an inch. NASCAR had figured this would take away the car's advantage, but it didn't. In fact, the following week, eight of the nine fastest cars were still Tauruses. So NASCAR made the Taurus rear spoiler even shorter, and this time it worked – Tauruses were equal to the Monte Carlo and Grand Prix models. By tweaking the rules between races, NASCAR officials kept the playing field fair and ensured a more exciting race for fans to watch.

Playing It Fair

Most of the changes to pre-existing rules are minor ones that only affect certain cars, like the rules concerning the Ford Taurus spoilers. The majority of the rules remain pretty consistent. For starters, the cars have to be "American-made steel-bodied passenger sedans," which is why you don't see German or Japanese cars racing in NASCAR, and also why drivers don't build their cars out of lighter metals like titanium. All teams have to follow the rules and cars are subject to inspection at almost any time to make sure that no team is trying to gain an unfair advantage. Some of the things the inspectors check are:

Engine: There are maximum size limits for each series; a Winston Cup engine can't be more than 358 cubic inches. NASCAR engines still use carburetors, as opposed to the fuel-injected engines found in most passenger cars today. This gives a stock car engine much more horsepower than a passenger car, with the downside being terrible gas mileage; in general, a race car averages about four miles to the gallon.

Gas Tank: The gas tank, known as the fuel cell, cannot hold more than 22 gallons of gas at a time. As a safety measure, the inside of the fuel cell has to be made of foam rubber so that it won't rupture and spill gasoline in the event of an accident.

Metal: Cars have to be made of steel, rather than lighter metals like titanium or aluminum. To make sure teams follow this rule, inspectors apply magnets to various parts of the car's body. If a magnet doesn't stick, they know a non-steel substitute is being used.

Body Shape: There are only three basic body shapes allowed, but a skillful engineer can make a car more aerodynamic by putting tiny, nearly invisible bumps or grooves on its body. The grooves serve to disrupt air flow in ways that either increase the car's aerodynamics or create turbulence for other cars on the track, both of which give an advantage to the modified version. NASCAR inspectors look for such things and also check the height of the rear spoiler.

Weight: Cars have to be a minimum weight to ensure that a lighter car doesn't have an advantage over a heavier competitor. A Winston Cup car, fully loaded with gas, oil and water, must weigh at least 3,400 pounds, with 1,600 pounds on the right side.

Height and Ground Clearance: Cars not only have to reach a minimum height, but the bottoms of the cars must be raised a certain distance off the ground. A car with either a lower height or a lower ground clearance would have an advantage over higher cars.

Tires: NASCAR officials don't actually inspect the tires, but in an effort to keep costs down, there is a maximum number of tires a driver can use, either during qualifying or during a race.

Playing It Safe

Not all of the rules are intended to ensure fairness; a lot of them are intended to protect the drivers in the event of a crash. Here are some of the things that inspectors typically look for to maintain safety standards:

Glass: There is no glass anywhere in a stock car. Headlights and brake lights are replaced with decals; there are no side windows and the front and back windshields are made of a shatterproof plastic called Lexan.

Belts and Nets: Five safety belts hold a driver in his seat and while strapping the belts on can take quite awhile, they can all be undone in a second by lifting a special latch so the driver can make a fast exit in the event of an emergency. Since there are no side windows in a car, the window opening is covered by a thick mesh net.

Roll Bars and Roll Cages: Roll bars, which are made of special steel tubing, are fashioned into a roll cage; a powerful framework that protects the driver in case his car rolls over.

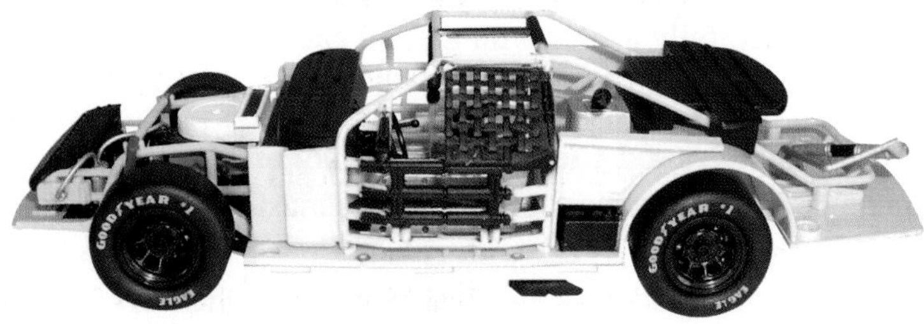

The Unfair Advantage

Despite the strict inspections, it is speculated that some drivers (or their teams) still try to get around the rules. Nowadays cars are weighed both before and after a race, but back in the 1970s that wasn't the case and so sometimes teams would think of ways to illegally reduce the weight of their cars. One trick involved a 26-pound lead brick disguised as a radio; after the car was weighed, the brick was discarded in favor of an actual radio. Even more notorious was the story of a driver in the 1978 season whose car started each race with nearly eighty pounds of buckshot that he discharged during the race. Inspectors never discovered the pellets or their hiding place, since every time the car would be jacked up for inspection the jack would cover the buckshot.

Follow The Flags

Most of the rules are more of a concern to the teams that work on cars than the drivers who pilot them. But drivers do have to pay attention to the flagman and memorize what the waving flags mean. Here are the eight types of flags used in NASCAR:

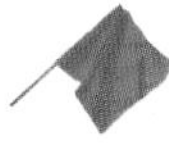

Green: The green flag is used to start the race or restart the race after a caution period.

Yellow: Yellow is the caution flag, which is used when there are dangerous conditions on the track. It is waved at the start/finish line and once a car crosses the line it must maintain its position rather than pass any other cars.

Red: Red flags are used when track conditions are so dangerous the race must stop. When the red flag is waved, all drivers must stop and no work or repairs can be done in the pits or garage.

Black: When a black flag is waved at a driver, he must report to his pit area immediately. This could be either because his car is hazardous or he's broken a rule.

Black With A White Cross: A driver who's been black-flagged can't continue driving, or else he'll get a black flag with a white cross, which means no more of his laps will be counted until he returns to the pits.

Blue With A Diagonal Orange Stripe: This is the passing flag and is waved to drivers who are down one lap or more. It signifies that they must yield to the lead lap cars about to pass them.

White: This flag is waved at the beginning of the last lap of the race.

Checkered: This flag means the race is over.

Anatomy Of A Race Car

The cars that NASCAR stars drive on the tracks are far different than the ones they use to travel to the grocery store on their days off. Though stock cars resemble regular cars, a closer look reveals a world of difference. The bottom line is that stock cars are built for speed and efficiency and they include safety features that are unnecessary in vehicles outside the world of Daytona or Talladega. Here is a brief rundown of some of the features you will find in a NASCAR race car:

1. **Roll Cage:** A structure built from steel tubing which surrounds the driver's area and protects him in the event of a crash.

2. **Roof Flaps:** Metal panels that open up when a car spins or travels backwards. They help prevent the car from flying off the ground in the event of a crash.

3. **Chassis:** The steel structure of a car, also known as its frame.

4. **Window Net:** Used in place of a window on the driver's side. Protects the driver from flying debris and helps him stay in the car during a crash.

5. **Lights:** The headlights and brake lights you see on stock cars are merely decals, added to make the cars look more like the cars you find on the road.

6. Restrictor Plates: Flat metal devices that lower horsepower and keep speeds down by decreasing the amount of air that reaches the carburetor. Restrictor plates are used when racing on superspeedways.

7. Carburetor: A device that mixes air and fuel for combustion in the engine. Allows for greater horsepower than fuel-injected engines.

8. Spoilers: Metal strips that assist in directing airflow, thus making the car more aerodynamic.

9. Fuel Cell: A 22-gallon fuel tank lined with a rubber "bladder" to help prevent dangerous spills and fires during crashes.

10. Sway Bar: Regulates the amount of the car's weight which is distributed to each of the car's springs during turns. The sway bar helps to balance the car and keep it moving quickly.

11. Track Bar: Attached to the rear axle and the car's frame, the track bar keeps the rear tires centered.

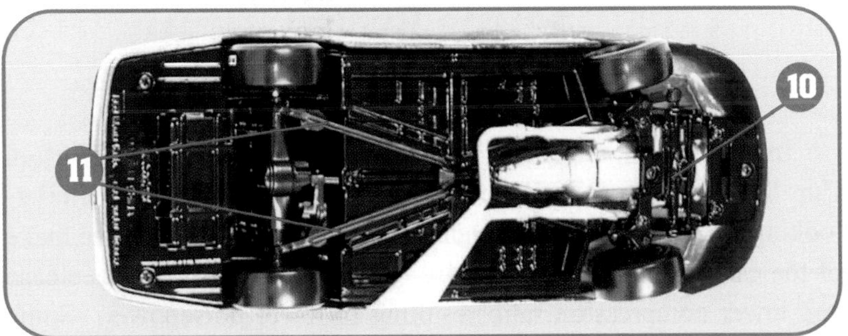

NASCAR® Series

Though the Winston Cup, Busch Grand National and Craftsman Truck are the best-known of the different NASCAR series, fans know that there's more to NASCAR than just these three. There are a total of 13 different series: the three already mentioned, nine in the NASCAR Touring Series and a Weekly Racing Series that is divided regionally. The different series are as follows:

Winston Cup Series

The Winston Cup is the most high-profile of all the NASCAR series. In its 1999 season, the Winston Cup Series held 34 races at various tracks throughout the United States. The Winston Cup tracks are some of the most formidable in racing. however, few drivers complain about the grueling schedule and the endless hours because the Winston Cup Championship is NASCAR's most prestigious award.

Busch Series, Grand National Division

In some ways, the Busch Series is a preparation for the Winston Cup Series. Both follow the same on-track rules and race similar-looking stock cars, with the fundamental difference being in the make of the cars. Busch Series cars are lighter, with a smaller wheelbase and lower compression ratio resulting in lower horsepower. Some drivers continue their Busch careers even after joining the Winston Cup Series, since most Busch races are held on Saturdays, while Winston Cup races are held on Sundays.

Craftsman Truck Series

NASCAR created the Craftsman Truck Series in 1994. Drivers say the Craftsman resembles the Winston Cup Series more than the Busch, since the trucks have almost as much horsepower as the Winston cars – 710 for each truck, compared to 750 for a Winston Cup car and 550 for a Busch car. Despite the similarities in power, the Craftsman Series' tracks, rules and appearances make it very different from the Winston Series (but just as thrilling).

Winston West Series

The Winston West Series originated in 1954 when NASCAR expanded to the West Coast. In recent years the Winston West Series has grown tremendously due to increased sponsorship and interest by the fans. The series ends with its final race in Montegi City, Japan. Winston West cars are virtually the same as Winston Cup cars except for some minor engine differences.

Busch North Series

Originally the NASCAR North tour, this series became the Busch North Series in 1987. The series has grown quickly and gained so much national recognition that in 2000 it will compete alongside the three national series. Busch North Series events are open to American-made, steel-bodied, passenger sedans from model years 1997-2000. The cars are similar to those in the Busch Grand National Division and only differ in weight.

Slim Jim All Pro Series

The Slim Jim All Pro Series is one of the four NASCAR regional touring series (in addition to the Featherlite Southwest, Raybestos Brakes Northwest and the Re/Max Challenge Series) to feature late-model cars and follow the same set of rules. Based in the Southeast, the division features cars such as the Buick LeSabre and Regal, Chevrolet Monte Carlo, Ford Taurus and Thunderbird, Oldsmobile Cutlass and Pontiac Grand Prix.

Featherlite Modified Series

The Featherlite Modified Series is one of NASCAR's oldest divisions and is also the only open-wheeled series in the touring division. In 1985, after modified race cars increased in popularity, NASCAR established this series for racing fans throughout the country.

Featherlite Southwest Series

The Featherlite Southwest Series started in 1986 and is one of the four regional touring series that share the same set of rules. 1999 saw several record-breaking moments in the series that are sure lead to increased fan awareness in upcoming years.

Goody's Dash Series

This series was established in 1975 for compact cars. In 1992, Goody's Pharmaceuticals took over the title sponsorship and the series is now known as the Goody's Dash Series. A regional series that is focused in the Southeast, it is the only series that competes at the Daytona International Speedway during the Speedweeks Festival in February. The compact cars used in the series are basically smaller versions of Winston Cup cars.

Raybestos Brakes Northwest Series

The Raybestos Brakes Northwest Series was created in 1985 for fans in the Pacific Northwest. The series uses cars that are only slightly smaller than the Winston Cup cars and in 1999 the series attracted many new fans during its tour. This is another of the four series that compete with the same set of rules.

Re/Max Challenge Series

The ARTGO Challenge Series was formed in 1975 and received a name change to the Re/Max Challenge Series in 1998. The Re/Max has earned a reputation for exciting racing throughout the Midwest. The series has been a companion event to the Busch Grand National, Craftsman Truck and Winston West Series.

Busch All-Star Series

Also known as the O'Reilly Auto Parts All-Star Series, this is the only dirt-track series in NASCAR. Races are held throughout the midwestern United States. The late model stock cars differ greatly from those used on the asphalt, and have no rules governing compression ratios.

NASCAR® Weekly Racing Series

The NASCAR Weekly Racing Series consists of both dirt and asphalt tracks nationwide. The racers have the opportunity to compete for over $1.7 million in awards in the various racing regions.

The Winner

In 1999, Weekly Racing Series racer Jeff Leka from the Heartland Region won a record $150,000. He won $149,950 in posted awards but received a fifty dollar bill from Tom Deery, Vice President of the Winston Racing Series who "didn't believe that any champion should win $149,950."

2000 Winston Cup Schedule

February

13	Bud Shootout @ Daytona Intl. Speedway	12:00 p.m.
17	Gatorade 125s @ Daytona Intl. Speedway	12:30 p.m.
20	Daytona 500 @ Daytona Intl. Speedway	12:00 p.m.
27	Dura-Lube/KMart 400 @ North Carolina Speedway	12:30 p.m.

March

5	Carsdirect.com 400 @ Las Vegas Motor Speedway	2:30 p.m.
12	Cracker Barrel Old Country Store 500 @ Atlanta Motor Speedway	1:00 p.m.
19	Mall.com 400 @ Darlington Raceway	12:30 p.m.
26	Food City 500 @ Bristol Motor Speedway	12:30 p.m.

April

2	DIRECTV 500 @ Texas Motor Speedway	2:00 p.m.
9	Goody's Body Pain 500 @ Martinsville Speedway	1:00 p.m.
16	DieHard 500 @ Talladega Superspeedway	1:00 p.m.
30	NAPA Auto Parts 500 @ California Speedway	2:00 p.m.

May

6	Pontiac Excitement 400 @ Richmond Intl. Raceway	7:30 p.m.
20	The Winston @ Lowe's Motor Speedway	7:30 p.m.
28	Coca-Cola 600 @ Lowe's Motor Speedway	6:05 p.m

June

4	MBNA Platinum 400 @ Dover Downs Intl. Speedway	12:30 p.m.
11	KMart 400 @ Michigan Speedway	1:00 p.m.
18	Pocono 500 @ Pocono Raceway	1:00 p.m.
25	Save Mart/Kragen 350K @ Sears Point Raceway	4:00 p.m.

July

1	Pepsi 400 @ Daytona Intl. Speedway	8:00 p.m.
9	Thatlook.com 300 @ New Hampshire Intl. Speedway	1:00 p.m.
23	Pennsylvania 500 @ Pocono Raceway	1:05 p.m.

August

5	Brickyard 400 @ Indianapolis Motor Speedway	1:00 p.m.
13	Global Crossing @ The Glen – Watkins Glen Intl.	12:30 p.m.
20	Pepsi 400 Presented by Meijer @ Michigan Speedway	1:00 p.m.
26	Goracing.com 500 @ Bristol Motor Speedway	7:30 p.m.

September

3	Southern 500 @ Darlington Raceway	1:00 p.m.
9	Chevrolet Monte Carlo 400 @ Richmond Intl. Spccdway	7:30 p.m.
17	New Hampshire 300 @ New Hampshire Intl. Speedway	12:30 p.m.
24	MBNA.com 400 @ Dover Downs Intl. Speedway	12:10 p.m.

October

1	NAPA Autocare 500 @ Martinsville Speedway	1:00 p.m.
8	UAW-GM Quality 500 @ Lowe's Motor Speedway	1:05 p.m.
15	Winston 500 @ Talladega Superspeedway	1:00 p.m.
22	Pop Secret Microwave Popcorn 400 @ North Carolina Speedway	12:30 p.m.

November

5	Checker Auto Parts/Dura Lube 500k @ Phoenix Intl. Raceway	2:00 p.m.
12	Pennzoil 400 @ Homestead-Miami Speedway	12:30 p.m.
19	Napa 500 @ Atlanta Motor Speedway	1:00 p.m.

Plan ahead for next year! Check our web site, ***CollectorsQuest.com***, for the 2001 Winston Cup schedule when it's available.

How To Use Your Collector's Value Guide™

1. Locate your car within each driver's section (drivers are listed alphabetically, while cars are listed chronologically by the year issued, and then alphabetically by name). Within each box, all manufacturers and scales for that model are listed in a grid format. An orange triangle (▲) indicates the manufacturer of the piece shown. (Please note that some of the photos are of the car in its box and that boxes do vary from manufacturer to manufacturer.) Occasionally, a special note which lists important facts or information about the car or driver can be found immediately below the manufacturer information. Space is given for you in the LE column to record any limited edition information about your piece. Blank lines are available in each box for writing in future releases, multiple-piece sets or other products such as die-cast banks or crystal cars.

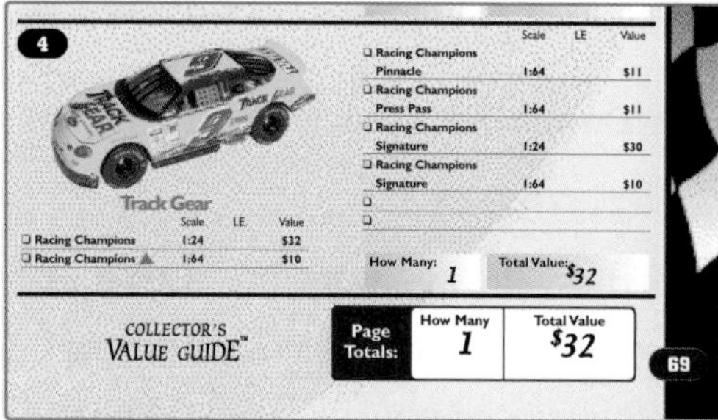

2. Record how many of each piece you have in the "How Many" box. Add up all of the values for each piece you have, and record that number in the "Total Value" box. Those die-cast cars that do not yet have a secondary market value are identified as "N/E" (not established). Now add up all of the "Total Value" boxes and record this value in the "Page Totals" box found at the bottom of each page. Do the same with your "How Many" totals.

3. Calculate the value of your entire collection by entering the values from the "Page Totals" boxes onto the corresponding lines of the "Total Value Of My Collection" pages at the back of the Value Guide. Add these numbers together and you will have the total value of your collection!

Jeff Burton

Jeff Burton has been a favorite with NASCAR fans ever since he started in the Busch Series in 1988. In Winston Cup races, he drives the #99 Ford sponsored by Exide Batteries, while *NorthernLight.com* recently began sponsoring him in the Busch series. In addition to his regular Exide paint scheme, Burton runs special promotional schemes from time to time; in recent years one of his most popular promotional paint schemes has been the Bruce Lee car which he ran at the 1996 exhibition race in Suzuka, Japan.

1992 Releases

1

TIC Financial

	Scale	LE	Value
❑ Matchbox/White Rose Super Stars	1:64		$8
❑ Racing Champions Promo ▲	1:64		$20
❑			
❑			
❑			
❑			

How Many: | Total Value:

1993 Releases

2

Baby Ruth

	Scale	LE	Value
❑ Matchbox/White Rose Super Stars ▲	1:64		$8
❑			
❑			
❑			
❑			

Note: On June 12, 1993, Jeff and Ward Burton were the first brothers to finish first and second in a Busch Grand National race, with Jeff coming in first.

How Many: | Total Value:

3

PHOTO UNAVAILABLE

TIC Financial

	Scale	LE	Value
❑ Matchbox/White Rose Super Stars	1:64		$8
❑			
❑			
❑			
❑			

How Many: | Total Value:

Page Totals:	How Many	Total Value

1994 Releases

4

Raybestos

	Scale	LE	Value
❑ Matchbox/White Rose Super Stars	1:64		$6
❑ Racing Champions (Goodyear tires)	1:24		$50
❑ Racing Champions (Hoosier tires)	1:24		$55
❑ Racing Champions	1:64		$13
❑ Racing Champions Premier ▲	1:64		$15
❑ Racing Champions Premier (yellow box)	1:64		$12
❑			

How Many: Total Value:

5

PHOTO UNAVAILABLE

TIC Financial

	Scale	LE	Value
❑ Matchbox/White Rose Future Cup Stars	1:64		$22
❑			
❑			
❑			
❑			

***Note:** Jeff Burton was the 1994 Winston Cup Rookie Of The Year award.*

How Many: Total Value:

1995 Releases

6

Raybestos

	Scale	LE	Value
❑ Matchbox/White Rose Super Stars	1:64		$6
❑ Racing Champions	1:24		$45
❑ Racing Champions (blue numbers)	1:64		$10
❑ Racing Champions (orange numbers) ▲	1:64		$10
❑ Racing Champions To The MAXX	1:64		$16
❑			

***Note:** In 1995, Burton had his first top 5 finish.*

How Many: Total Value:

7

PHOTO UNAVAILABLE

Raybestos (gold)

	Scale	LE	Value
❑ Matchbox/White Rose Super Star Awards	1:64		$32
❑			
❑			
❑			
❑			

***Note:** Jeff Burton began his racing career at the age of 7, racing go-karts at the speedway in South Boston, Virginia.*

How Many: Total Value:

Page Totals:	How Many	Total Value

1996 Releases

8

Exide

	Scale	LE	Value
❑ Action	1:24		$85
❑ Action ▲	1:64		$14
❑ Matchbox/White Rose Super Stars	1:64		$6
❑ Racing Champions	1:24		$40
❑ Racing Champions	1:64		$13
❑ Revell	1:24		$25
❑ Revell	1:64		$7
❑ Revell Collection	1:24		$52
❑ Revell Collection	1:64		$17
❑			

How Many: Total Value:

9

PHOTO UNAVAILABLE

Raybestos

	Scale	LE	Value
❑ Ertl	1:18		$60
❑			
❑			
❑			
❑			
❑			

Note: 1996 marked Burton's first pole position in a Winston Cup race.

How Many: Total Value:

1997 Releases

10

Exide

	Scale	LE	Value
❑ Action	1:24		$70
❑ Action (Mac Tools) ▲	1:24		N/E
❑ Action	1:64		$14
❑ Action/RCCA	1:64		$24
❑ Action/RCCA Elite	1:24		$175
❑ Ertl (Dealer Only)	1:18		N/E
❑ Hot Wheels	1:64		$6
❑ Hot Wheels Collector	1:64		$8
❑ Hot Wheels Short Track	1:64		$8
❑ Hot Wheels Superspeedway	1:64		$8
❑ Racing Champions	1:24		$38
❑ Racing Champions	1:64		$12
❑ Racing Champions	1:144		$7
❑ Racing Champions Pinnacle	1:64		$14
❑ Racing Champions Premier with emblem	1:64		$15
❑ Racing Champions Preview	1:64		$13
❑ Revell Collection	1:24		$63
❑ Revell Collection (Texas Win)	1:24		$75
❑ Revell Collection	1:43		$42
❑ Revell Select	1:24		$40
❑			
❑			
❑			
❑			

Note: Jeff Burton won the first Winston Cup race held at Texas Motor Speedway, on April 6, 1997.

How Many: Total Value:

11

Exide

	Scale	LE	Value
❑ Racing Champions Chrome Chase ▲	1:64		N/E
❑			
❑			
❑			
❑			

How Many: Total Value:

12

Track Gear

	Scale	LE	Value
❑ Action	1:64		$13
❑ Action/RCCA ▲	1:24		$65
❑ Action/RCCA	1:64		$22
❑ Action/RCCA Elite	1:24		$125
❑ Racing Champions	1:64		$12
❑			
❑			
❑			
❑			

Note: In 1997, Jeff Burton finished fourth in the Winston Cup point standings.

How Many: Total Value:

1998 Releases

13

Exide

	Scale	LE	Value
❑ Hot Wheels Collector ▲	1:64		$6
❑ Hot Wheels Preview	1:64		$7
❑ Hot Wheels Track Edition	1:64		$12
❑ Hot Wheels Trading Paint	1:64		$14
❑ Racing Champions	1:24		$29
❑ Racing Champions	1:64		$12
❑ Racing Champions Authentics	1:24		$84
❑ Racing Champions Press Pass	1:64		$17
❑ Racing Champions Preview	1:144		N/E
❑ Racing Champions Roaring Racers	1:64		N/E
❑ Racing Champions Signature Driver Series	1:24		$35
❑ Racing Champions Signature Driver Series	1:64		$12
❑			
❑			
❑			
❑			

Note: In 1998, Burton drove into Victory Lane twice and had 18 top-five finishes and 23 top ten finishes.

How Many: Total Value:

Page Totals:	How Many	Total Value

14

Exide

	Scale	LE	Value
❑ Racing Champions Chrome Chase ▲	1:64		$65

	Scale	LE	Value
❑			
❑			
❑			
❑			

Note: *In 1998, Jeff Burton won the Chevrolet Monte Carlo 400.*

How Many: Total Value:

15

Exide

	Scale	LE	Value
❑ Racing Champions Gold	1:24		$90

	Scale	LE	Value
❑ Racing Champions Gold (hood open)	1:24		$70
❑ Racing Champions Gold with emblem	1:64		$30
❑ Racing Champions Reflections in Gold	1:24		$68
❑ Racing Champions Reflections in Gold	1:64		$30
❑ Racing Champions Gold Chrome (Toys 'R Us) ▲	1:64		$14
❑			

How Many: Total Value:

16

Exide

	Scale	LE	Value
❑ Hot Wheels Test Track ▲	1:64		$10
❑			

	Scale	LE	Value
❑			
❑			
❑			
❑			

Note: *Jeff Burton won the Jiffy Lube 300 in 1997, 1998 and 1999.*

How Many: Total Value:

17

Track Gear

	Scale	LE	Value
❑ Racing Champions	1:24		$32
❑ Racing Champions ▲	1:64		$10

	Scale	LE	Value
❑ Racing Champions Pinnacle	1:64		$11
❑ Racing Champions Press Pass	1:64		$11
❑ Racing Champions Signature Driver Series	1:24		$30
❑ Racing Champions Signature Driver Series	1:64		$10
❑			
❑			

How Many: Total Value:

Page Totals:	How Many	Total Value

18

Track Gear

	Scale	LE	Value
❑ Racing Champions Chrome Chase ▲	1:64		$60

	Scale	LE	Value
❑			
❑			
❑			
❑			

How Many: Total Value:

19

PHOTO UNAVAILABLE

Track Gear

	Scale	LE	Value
❑ Racing Champions Gold with emblem	1:64		$25

	Scale	LE	Value
❑ Racing Champions Reflections in Gold	1:64		$25
❑			
❑			
❑			
❑			

How Many: Total Value:

1999 Releases

20

Bruce Lee

	Scale	LE	Value
❑ Race Image Dimension 4	1:32		$10
❑ Racing Champions ▲	1:24		$33

	Scale	LE	Value
❑ Racing Champions	1:64		$15
❑ Racing Champions Authentics	1:24		$30
❑ Racing Champions NASCAR Rules!	1:64		$24
❑			
❑			

How Many: Total Value:

21

Bruce Lee

	Scale	LE	Value
❑ Racing Champions Chrome Chase (Toys 'R Us) ▲	1:64		N/E

	Scale	LE	Value
❑			
❑			
❑			
❑			

Note: In 1999, Jeff Burton placed fifth in the Winston Cup point standings for the second consecutive year, after six victories, 18 finishes in the top five and 23 finishes in the top ten.

How Many: Total Value:

Page Totals:	How Many	Total Value

22

Bruce Lee

	Scale	LE	Value
❑ Racing Champions Gold ▲	1:24		$48
❑ Racing Champions Gold Chrome (Target Exclusive)	1:24		N/E
❑			
❑			
❑			
❑			

Note: *Burton's Bruce Lee car was a special paint scheme for a promotional race in Japan.*

How Many: | Total Value:

23

Exide

	Scale	LE	Value
❑ Hot Wheels ▲	1:24		$25
❑ Hot Wheels Collector	1:64		$8
❑ Hot Wheels Crew's Choice	1:24		$45
❑ Hot Wheels Crew's Choice	1:43		$28
❑ Hot Wheels Deluxe Black Chrome	1:24		N/E
❑ Hot Wheels Track Edition	1:64		N/E
❑ Racing Champions	1:24		$28
❑ Racing Champions	1:64		$10
❑ Racing Champions NASCAR Rules!	1:64		$24
❑ Racing Champions Press Pass	1:64		$17
❑ Racing Champions Signature Driver Series	1:24		$33
❑ Racing Champions Signature Driver Series (silver stripe)	1:24		N/E
❑ Racing Champions Signature Driver Series (silver stripe)	1:64		$11
❑ Racing Champions Under The Lights (silver stripe)	1:24		$40
❑ Racing Champions Under The Lights (silver stripe)	1:64		$18
❑ Team Caliber (No Bull)	1:24		$130
❑ Team Caliber	1:64		$26
❑			
❑			
❑			
❑			

Note: *Burton finished first in the 1999 TransSouth Financial 400 held on March 21, 1999.*

How Many: | Total Value:

24

Exide

	Scale	LE	Value
❑ Racing Champions Authentics ▲	1:24		$88
❑			
❑			
❑			
❑			

Note: *This car features Burton's 1998 paint scheme.*

How Many: | Total Value:

Page Totals:	How Many	Total Value

25

Exide

	Scale	LE	Value
❑ Racing Champions 24K Gold ▲	1:24		$56

	Scale	LE	Value
❑ Racing Champions 24K Gold	1:64		$24
❑ Racing Champions Gold	1:24		$35
❑ Racing Champions Gold	1:64		$22
❑			
❑			
❑			
❑			

How Many: Total Value:

26

PHOTO UNAVAILABLE

Exide

	Scale	LE	Value
❑ Racing Champions Platinum	1:24		$55

	Scale	LE	Value
❑ Racing Champions Platinum	1:64		$24
❑			
❑			
❑			
❑			

Note: During the Dura Lube/Big K 400, Jeff Burton won the True Value Hard Charger Of The Race Award.

How Many: Total Value:

27

PHOTO UNAVAILABLE

Exide

	Scale	LE	Value
❑ Hot Wheels Test Track	1:64		$20
❑			

	Scale	LE	Value
❑			
❑			
❑			
❑			

Note: In 1999, Burton won the Carsdirect.com 400.

How Many: Total Value:

28

Track Gear

	Scale	LE	Value
❑ Racing Champions Authentics ▲	1:24		$74

	Scale	LE	Value
❑ Racing Champions NASCAR Rules!	1:64		$17
❑ Racing Champions Press Pass	1:64		$13
❑			
❑			
❑			
❑			

How Many: Total Value:

Page Totals:	How Many	Total Value

29

Track Gear

	Scale	LE	Value
❑ Racing Champions 24K Gold	1:24		$55
❑ Racing Champions 24K Gold	1:64		$22
❑			
❑			
❑			
❑			

How Many: | Total Value:

30

Track Gear

	Scale	LE	Value
❑ Racing Champions Platinum	1:24		$75
❑ Racing Champions Platinum	1:64		$20
❑			
❑			
❑			
❑			

How Many: | Total Value:

2000 Releases

31

Exide

	Scale	LE	Value
❑ Hot Wheels	1:64		$5
❑ Hot Wheels Crew's Choice	1:24		$38
❑ Hot Wheels Crew's Choice	1:64		$10
❑ Hot Wheels Deluxe	1:24		$30
❑ Hot Wheels Deluxe	1:43		$27
❑ Hot Wheels Deluxe ▲	1:64		$8
❑ Hot Wheels Select	1:24		$30
❑ Hot Wheels Select	1:43		$28
❑ Hot Wheels Select	1:64		$8
❑ Hot Wheels Track Edition	1:64		$12
❑ Racing Champions	1:24		$25
❑ Racing Champions	1:64		$8
❑ Racing Champions NASCAR Rules!	1:64		$12
❑ Racing Champions Premier	1:24		$40
❑ Racing Champions Premier	1:64		$12
❑ Racing Champions Premier Preview	1:64		$12
❑ Racing Champions Preview	1:24		$27
❑ Racing Champions Preview	1:64		$10
❑ Racing Champions War Paint	1:24		$30
❑ Racing Champions War Paint	1:64		$11
❑ Team Caliber Owner's Series	1:24		$95
❑ Team Caliber Owner's Series	1:64		$20
❑ Team Caliber Preferred	1:24		$80
❑ Team Caliber White Knuckles	1:64		$12
❑			

Note: Jeff Burton won the Pepsi 400 on July 4, 2000.

How Many: | Total Value:

Page Totals:	How Many	Total Value

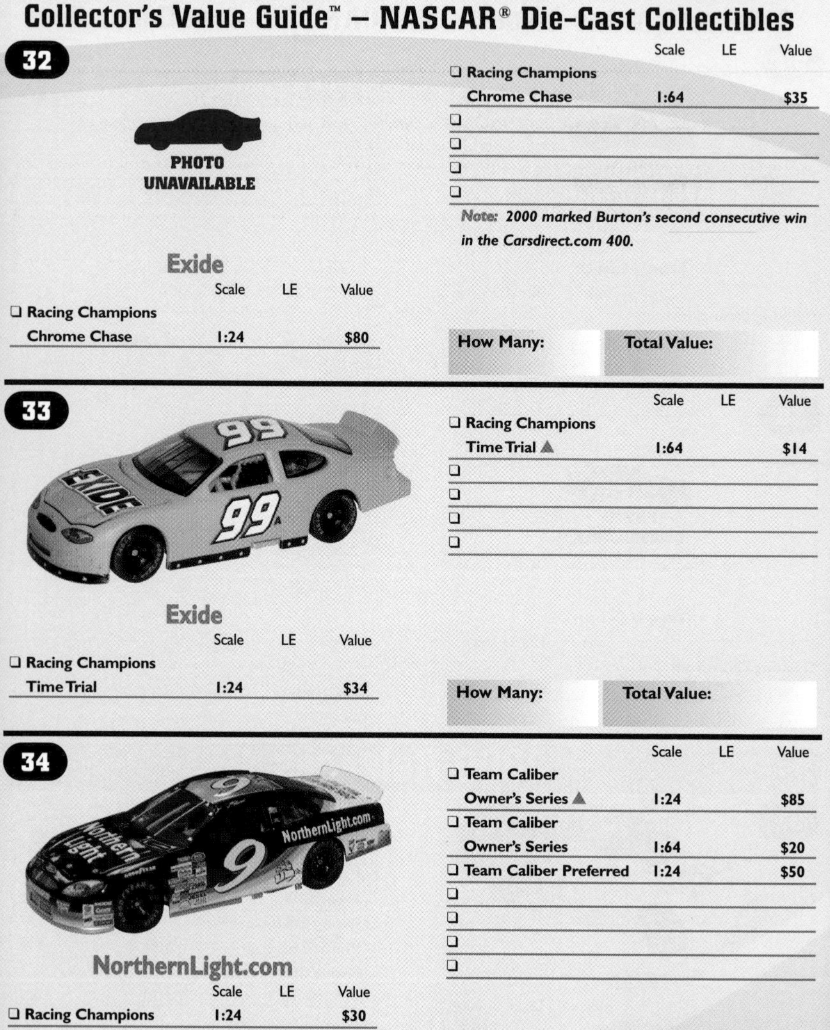

32

PHOTO UNAVAILABLE

Exide

	Scale	LE	Value
❑ Racing Champions Chrome Chase	1:24		$80

	Scale	LE	Value
❑ Racing Champions Chrome Chase	1:64		$35
❑			
❑			
❑			
❑			

Note: 2000 marked Burton's second consecutive win in the Carsdirect.com 400.

How Many: Total Value:

33

Exide

	Scale	LE	Value
❑ Racing Champions Time Trial	1:24		$34

	Scale	LE	Value
❑ Racing Champions Time Trial ▲	1:64		$14
❑			
❑			
❑			
❑			

How Many: Total Value:

34

NorthernLight.com

	Scale	LE	Value
❑ Racing Champions	1:24		$30

	Scale	LE	Value
❑ Team Caliber Owner's Series ▲	1:24		$85
❑ Team Caliber Owner's Series	1:64		$20
❑ Team Caliber Preferred	1:24		$50
❑			
❑			
❑			
❑			

How Many: Total Value:

Page Totals:	How Many	Total Value

Future Releases

Check our web site, ***CollectorsQuest.com***, for new Jeff Burton product releases and record the information here.

Jeff Burton	Value	How Many	Total Value

Page Totals:	How Many	Total Value

Future Releases

Check our web site, ***CollectorsQuest.com***, for new Jeff Burton product releases and record the information here.

Jeff Burton	Value	How Many	Total Value

Page Totals:	How Many	Total Value

Dale Earnhardt®

Although most of his current cars are black, Dale Earnhardt has had many different paint schemes. His 1995 "Winston Silver Select" car is credited with starting the paint-scheme craze, while his 2000 car designed by Peter Max may be one of the most colorful paint schemes in NASCAR history. Earnhardt has also driven a number of cars featuring the Tasmanian Devil, however, he can most often be seen driving a car sponsored by Goodwrench.

1989 Releases

1

PHOTO UNAVAILABLE

Goodwrench

	Scale	LE	Value
❑ Racing Champions	1:64		$170
❑			

	Scale	LE	Value
❑			
❑			
❑			
❑			

How Many: | Total Value:

1990 Releases

2

Goodwrench

	Scale	LE	Value
❑ Matchbox/White Rose Super Stars	1:64		$60

	Scale	LE	Value
❑ Racing Champions (Goodwrench on trunk)	1:64		$280
❑ Racing Champions (Performance Parts)	1:64		$110
❑			
❑			
❑			

▲ *Pictured car is part of a collector's set.*

How Many: | Total Value:

1991 Releases

3

Goodwrench

	Scale	LE	Value
❑ Matchbox (Quick Lube)	1:64		$40

	Scale	LE	Value
❑ Matchbox (Western Steer) ▲	1:64		$29
❑ Racing Champions	1:64		$220
❑			
❑			
❑			
❑			

How Many: | Total Value:

Page Totals:	How Many	Total Value

1992 Releases

4

Goodwrench

	Scale	LE	Value
❑ Ertl	1:18		$150

	Scale	LE	Value
❑ Matchbox/White Rose Super Stars (Mom 'n' Pops)	1:64		$12
❑ Matchbox/White Rose Super Stars (no stripes) ▲	1:64		$15
❑ Racing Champions (stickers)	1:24		$150
❑ Racing Champions (tampo printing)	1:24		$150
❑ Racing Champions Premier	1:43		$40
❑ Racing Champions Premier	1:64		$30

How Many: Total Value:

1993 Releases

5

Goodwrench

	Scale	LE	Value
❑ Racing Champions (Mom 'n' Pops)	1:24		$80

	Scale	LE	Value
❑ Racing Champions (white fender)	1:24		$75
❑ Racing Champions (yellow fender)	1:24		$75
❑ Racing Champions	1:43		$30
❑ Racing Champions	1:64		$25
❑ Racing Champions Premier	1:43		$80
❑ Revell (6-Time)	1:24		$40
❑ Revell/Sports Image	1:24		$30

▲ *Pictured car is the 1998 release.*

How Many: Total Value:

6

Goodwrench

	Scale	LE	Value
❑ Racing Champions	1:64		$33
❑			

	Scale	LE	Value
❑			
❑			
❑			
❑			

▲ *Pictured car is the 1995 release.*

Note: This is a model of Dale Earnhardt's 1988 Monte Carlo.

How Many: Total Value:

7

PHOTO UNAVAILABLE

Goodwrench

	Scale	LE	Value
❑ Racing Champions	1:64		$58
❑			

	Scale	LE	Value
❑			
❑			
❑			
❑			

Note: This is a model of Earnhardt's 1989 Monte Carlo Fastback.

How Many: Total Value:

Page Totals:	How Many	Total Value

1994 Releases

8

Goodwrench

	Scale	LE	Value
❑ Action	1:64		$40
❑ Action (BGN)	1:64		$25
❑ Action/RCCA ▲	1:24		$350
❑ Action/RCCA	1:64		$30
❑ Action/RCCA (BGN)	1:64		$48
❑ Matchbox/White Rose Super Stars	1:64		$15
❑ Racing Champions Premier	1:43		$60
❑ Racing Champions Premier	1:64		$12
❑ Racing Champions Premier (Brickyard 400)	1:64		$55
❑ Revell	1:24		$30
❑ Sports Image (Kellogg's, BGN)	1:24		N/E

How Many: Total Value:

9

Goodwrench

	Scale	LE	Value
❑ Action	1:64		$60
❑			
❑			
❑			
❑			
❑			

▲ *Pictured car is the 1995 release.*

Note: *This is a model of Earnhardt's 1988 car.*

How Many: Total Value:

10

Goodwrench

	Scale	LE	Value
❑ Matchbox/White Rose Super Stars ▲	1:64		$40
❑			
❑			
❑			
❑			

Note: *This is a model of Earnhardt's 1993 car.*

How Many: Total Value:

11

Wrangler

	Scale	LE	Value
❑ Action/RCCA	1:64		$55
❑			
❑			
❑			
❑			
❑			

▲ *Pictured car is the 1995 release.*

Note: *This is a model of Earnhardt's 1985 Wrangler.*

How Many: Total Value:

COLLECTOR'S VALUE GUIDE™

Page Totals:	How Many	Total Value

12

Wrangler

	Scale	LE	Value
❑ Action/RCCA	1:24		N/E
❑ Action/RCCA	1:64		$60

	Scale	LE	Value
❑			
❑			
❑			
❑			

▲ *Pictured car is the 1995 release.*

Note: *This is a model of Earnhardt's 1987 Wrangler.*

How Many: **Total Value:**

1995 Releases

13

Goodwrench

	Scale	LE	Value
❑ Action	1:24		$135
❑ Action (Brickyard 400)	1:24		$110
❑ Action (w/card, Brickyard 400)	1:24		$140
❑ Action	1:64		N/E
❑ Action (Brickyard 400)	1:64		$23
❑ Action/RCCA (w/headlights)	1:24		$250
❑ Action/RCCA (w/out headlights) ▲	1:24		$285
❑ Action/RCCA	1:64		N/E
❑ Action/RCCA (black window)	1:64		$38
❑ Ertl	1:18		$75
❑ Matchbox/White Rose Super Stars	1:64		$8
❑ Matchbox/White Rose Super Stars (7-time champ)	1:64		$45
❑			
❑			
❑			
❑			

How Many: **Total Value:**

14

Goodwrench

	Scale	LE	Value
❑ Action/RCCA ▲	1:24		$625
❑			
❑			
❑			
❑			
❑			

Note: *This is a model of Earnhardt's 1988 car.*

How Many: **Total Value:**

Page Totals:	How Many	Total Value

15

Winston Silver Select

	Scale	LE	Value
❑ Action ▲	1:24		$975
❑ Action	1:64		$85
❑ Action (GM Parts)	1:64		$600
❑ Action (LE-20,000)	1:64		N/E
❑ Action Promo	1:64		$85
❑ Action/RCCA	1:64		$130
❑ Ertl	1:18		$175
❑			
❑			
❑			
❑			

How Many: Total Value:

16

Wrangler

	Scale	LE	Value
❑ Action ▲	1:24		$325
❑ Action	1:64		$50
❑ Action/RCCA	1:64		$44
❑			
❑			
❑			
❑			

Note: *This is a model of Earnhardt's 1981 car.*

How Many: Total Value:

17

Wrangler

	Scale	LE	Value
❑ Action ▲	1:24		$295
❑ Action/RCCA	1:64		$50
❑			
❑			
❑			
❑			

Note: *This is a model of Earnhardt's 1981 Wrangler.*

How Many: Total Value:

18

Wrangler

	Scale	LE	Value
❑ Action/RCCA	1:64		$40
❑			
❑			
❑			
❑			
❑			

▲ *Pictured car is the 1996 release.*

Note: *This is a model of Earnhardt's 1982 car.*

How Many: Total Value:

Page Totals:	How Many	Total Value

19

Wrangler

	Scale	LE	Value
❑ Action	1:24		$245
❑ Action/RCCA	1:64		$15

	Scale	LE	Value
❑			
❑			
❑			
❑			

▲ *Pictured car is part of a collector's set.*

***Note:** This is a model of Earnhardt's 1983 Wrangler.*

How Many: | Total Value:

20

Wrangler

	Scale	LE	Value
❑ Action	1:64		$60
❑ Action/RCCA	1:24		$335

	Scale	LE	Value
❑			
❑			
❑			
❑			

▲ *Pictured car is part of a collector's set.*

***Note:** This is a model of Earnhardt's 1984 Wrangler.*

How Many: | Total Value:

21

Wrangler

	Scale	LE	Value
❑ Action ▲	1:24		$270
❑			

	Scale	LE	Value
❑			
❑			
❑			
❑			

***Note:** This is a model of Earnhardt's 1985 car.*

How Many: | Total Value:

22

Wrangler

	Scale	LE	Value
❑ Action ▲	1:24		$400
❑			

	Scale	LE	Value
❑			
❑			
❑			
❑			

***Note:** This is a model of Earnhardt's 1987 car.*

How Many: | Total Value:

Page Totals:	How Many	Total Value

1996 Releases

23

ACDelco

	Scale	LE	Value
❑ Action	1:24		$52
❑ Action ▲	1:64		$19
❑ Action/RCCA	1:24		$95
❑ Action/RCCA	1:64		$38
❑ Brookfield	1:25		N/E
❑			
❑			
❑			
❑			

How Many: Total Value:

24

Goodwrench

	Scale	LE	Value
❑ Action ▲	1:64		$15
❑ Action/RCCA	1:64		$26
❑ Revell	1:64		$10
❑			
❑			
❑			
❑			

How Many: Total Value:

25

Olympics

	Scale	LE	Value
❑ Action	1:24		$55
❑ Action (Food City)	1:24		$115
❑ Action (Goodwrench box)	1:24		$100
❑ Action (green box)	1:24		$150
❑ Action (Mom 'n' Pops)	1:24		$100
❑ Action ▲	1:64		$24
❑ Action (black window)	1:64		$20
❑ Action/RCCA	1:64		$55
❑ Action/Sports Image	1:24		$75
❑ Revell	1:24		$28
❑ Revell	1:64		$30
❑ Revell Collection	1:24		$60
❑			

How Many: Total Value:

26

Winston Silver Select

	Scale	LE	Value
❑ Brookfield	1:25		$200
❑			
❑			
❑			
❑			
❑			

▲ *Pictured car is the 1995 release.*

Note: *This is a model of Earnhardt's 1995 car.*

How Many: Total Value:

Page Totals:	How Many	Total Value

27

Wrangler

	Scale	LE	Value
❑ Action	1:24		$130
❑ Action/RCCA ▲	1:24		$135

	Scale	LE	Value
❑			
❑			
❑			
❑			

Note: *This is a model of Earnhardt's 1982 car.*

How Many: | **Total Value:**

1997 Releases

28

ACDelco

	Scale	LE	Value
❑ Action/RCCA Elite ▲	1:24		$85
❑			

	Scale	LE	Value
❑			
❑			
❑			
❑			

How Many: | **Total Value:**

29

ACDelco

	Scale	LE	Value
❑ Action	1:64		$15
❑ Action (hood open)	1:64		$20

	Scale	LE	Value
❑ Winner's Circle	1:24		$30
❑ Winner's Circle Lifetime Series	1:64		$75
❑			
❑			
❑			
❑			

▲ *Pictured car is the 1996 release.*

Note: *This is a model of Earnhardt's 1996 car.*

How Many: | **Total Value:**

30

Goodwrench

	Scale	LE	Value
❑ Action	1:64		$27
❑ Action/RCCA	1:24		$220

	Scale	LE	Value
❑ Action/RCCA	1:64		$30
❑ Action/RCCA Elite ▲	1:24		$435
❑ Winner's Circle	1:24		$35
❑ Winner's Circle	1:64		$13
❑ Winner's Circle Lifetime Series	1:64		$40
❑			
❑			
❑			
❑			

How Many: | **Total Value:**

Page Totals:	How Many	Total Value

31

Goodwrench

	Scale	LE	Value
❑ Winner's Circle Lifetime Series	1:64		$28

	Scale	LE	Value
❑			
❑			
❑			
❑			

▲ *Pictured car is part of a collector's set.*

Note: *This is a model of Earnhardt's 1990 Goodwrench car.*

How Many: **Total Value:**

32

Goodwrench Plus

	Scale	LE	Value
❑ Action	1:24		$80
❑ Action (Brickyard 400)	1:24		$85

	Scale	LE	Value
❑ Action (Parts Plus)	1:24		N/E
❑ Action	1:64		$20
❑ Action (Brickyard 400)	1:64		$25
❑ Action/RCCA	1:64		$40
❑ Action/RCCA Elite ▲	1:24		$135
❑ Winner's Circle	1:24		$13
❑ Winner's Circle	1:64		N/E
❑			
❑			
❑			

How Many: **Total Value:**

33

Lowes Foods

	Scale	LE	Value
❑ Action/RCCA	1:24		$128

	Scale	LE	Value
❑ Winner's Circle Lifetime Series	1:64		N/E
❑			
❑			
❑			
❑			

▲ *Pictured car is part of a collector's set.*

Note: *This is a model of Earnhardt's 1989 Lowes Foods car.*

How Many: **Total Value:**

34

Mike Curb

	Scale	LE	Value
❑ Winner's Circle Lifetime Series ▲	1:64		$34

	Scale	LE	Value
❑			
❑			
❑			
❑			

Note: *This is a model of Earnhardt's 1980 car.*

How Many: **Total Value:**

Page Totals:	How Many	Total Value

35

Rod Osterlund

	Scale	LE	Value
❑ Winner's Circle Lifetime Series ▲	1:64		$34

	Scale	LE	Value
❑			
❑			
❑			
❑			

***Note:** This is a model of Earnhardt's 1978 car.*

How Many: **Total Value:**

36

RPM

	Scale	LE	Value
❑ Winner's Circle Lifetime Series ▲	1:64		$23

	Scale	LE	Value
❑			
❑			
❑			
❑			

***Note:** This is a model of Earnhardt's 1975 RPM car.*

How Many: **Total Value:**

37

Wheaties

	Scale	LE	Value
❑ Action ▲	1:24		$185
❑ Action (mail-in)	1:24		$70
❑ Action (Snap-On)	1:24		$200
❑ Action	1:64		$35
❑ Action/RCCA	1:64		$65
❑ Action/RCCA (black window)	1:64		N/E
❑ Action/RCCA Elite (gold number)	1:24		$335
❑ Action/RCCA Elite (second run)	1:24		$200
❑ Action/Sports Image	1:24		$90
❑ Revell Collection	1:18		$195
❑ Winner's Circle	1:24		$20
❑ Winner's Circle Lifetime Series	1:24		$30
❑			

	Scale	LE	Value
❑			
❑			
❑			
❑			

How Many: **Total Value:**

Page Totals:	How Many	Total Value

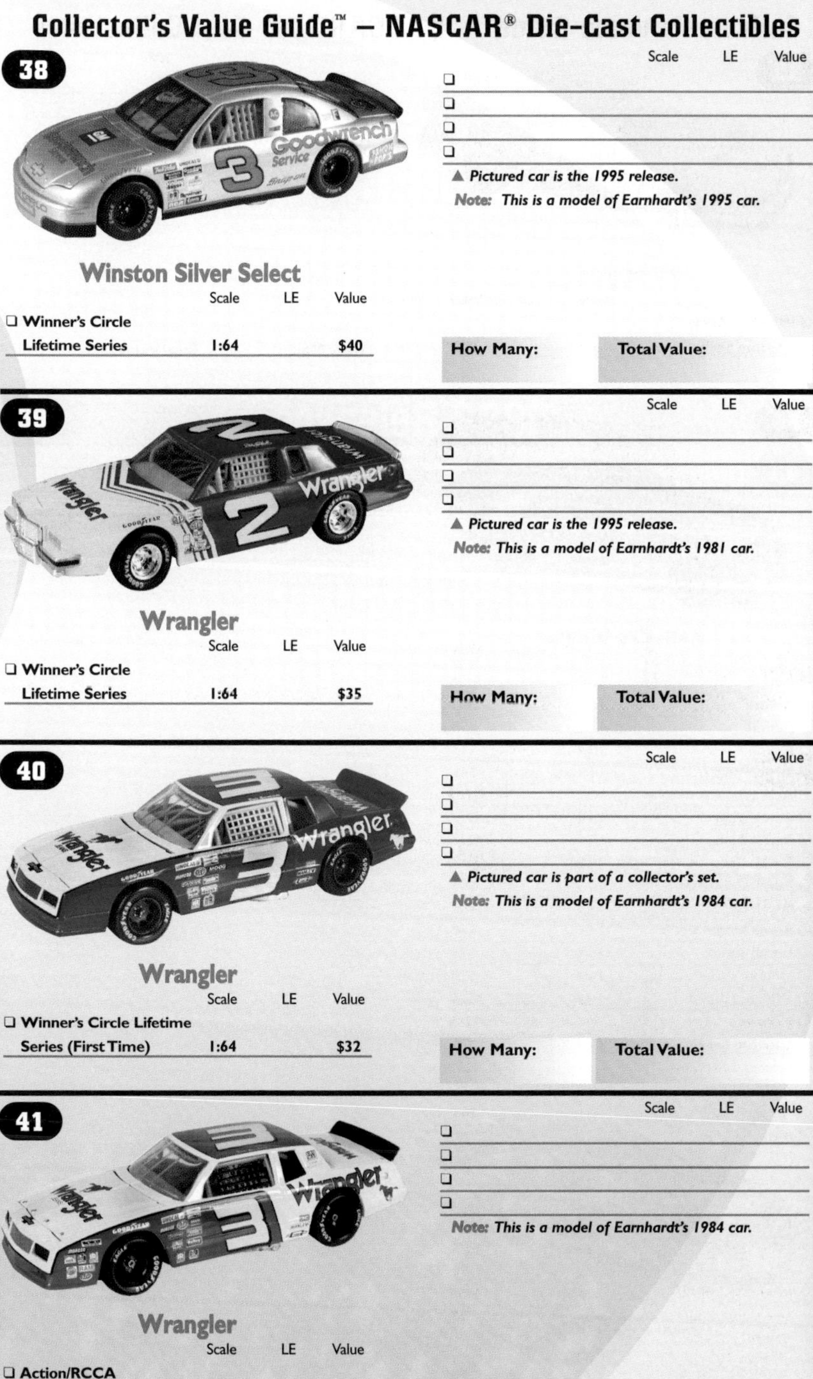

38

Winston Silver Select

	Scale	LE	Value
❑ Winner's Circle Lifetime Series	1:64		$40

	Scale	LE	Value
❑			
❑			
❑			
❑			

▲ *Pictured car is the 1995 release.*

***Note:** This is a model of Earnhardt's 1995 car.*

How Many: **Total Value:**

39

Wrangler

	Scale	LE	Value
❑ Winner's Circle Lifetime Series	1:64		$35

	Scale	LE	Value
❑			
❑			
❑			
❑			

▲ *Pictured car is the 1995 release.*

***Note:** This is a model of Earnhardt's 1981 car.*

How Many: **Total Value:**

40

Wrangler

	Scale	LE	Value
❑ Winner's Circle Lifetime Series (First Time)	1:64		$32

	Scale	LE	Value
❑			
❑			
❑			
❑			

▲ *Pictured car is part of a collector's set.*

***Note:** This is a model of Earnhardt's 1984 car.*

How Many: **Total Value:**

41

Wrangler

	Scale	LE	Value
❑ Action/RCCA (Daytona 500) ▲	1:24		$205

	Scale	LE	Value
❑			
❑			
❑			
❑			

***Note:** This is a model of Earnhardt's 1984 car.*

How Many: **Total Value:**

Page Totals:	How Many	Total Value

42

Wrangler

	Scale	LE	Value
❑ Winner's Circle Lifetime Series	1:64		$28

	Scale	LE	Value
❑			
❑			
❑			
❑			

▲ *Pictured car is part of a collector's set.*

Note: *This is a model of Earnhardt's 1986 car.*

How Many: **Total Value:**

1998 Releases

43

Bass Pro Shops

	Scale	LE	Value
❑ Action	1:18		$135
❑ Action	1:24		$125
❑ Action	1:32		$50
❑ Action	1:64		$23
❑ Action/RCCA	1:64		$45
❑ Action/RCCA Elite ▲	1:24		$200
❑ Revell Club	1:18		$215
❑ Revell Club	1:24		$125
❑ Revell Collection	1:18		$100
❑ Revell Collection	1:24		$90
❑ Revell Collection	1:43		$60
❑ Revell Select	1:24		$40
❑ Revell Select	1:64		$28
❑ Winner's Circle	1:24		$30
❑ Winner's Circle	1:43		$16
❑ Winner's Circle Lifetime Series	1:64		$7

	Scale	LE	Value
❑			
❑			
❑			
❑			

How Many: **Total Value:**

44

Bass Pro Shops

	Scale	LE	Value
❑ Action/RCCA ▲	1:32		$85
❑ Action/RCCA Elite	1:24		$1,350

	Scale	LE	Value
❑			
❑			
❑			
❑			

How Many: **Total Value:**

Page Totals:	How Many	Total Value

45

Coca-Cola

	Scale	LE	Value
❑ Action	1:18		$100
❑ Action	1:24		$55
❑ Action	1:64		$18
❑ Action/RCCA	1:64		$30
❑ Action/RCCA Elite ▲	1:24		$185
❑ Revell Club	1:18		$160
❑ Revell Club	1:24		$110
❑ Revell Collection	1:18		$115
❑ Revell Collection	1:24		$72
❑ Revell Collection	1:43		$36
❑ Revell Collection	1:64		$23
❑ Winner's Circle	1:24		$14
❑ Winner's Circle	1:64		$11
❑			

How Many: | Total Value:

46

Goodwrench

	Scale	LE	Value
❑ Winner's Circle Lifetime Series	1:64		$20
❑			
❑			
❑			
❑			

▲ *Pictured car is the 1995 release.*

Note: *This is a model of Earnhardt's 1988 car.*

How Many: | Total Value:

47

Goodwrench

	Scale	LE	Value
❑ Winner's Circle Silver Series ▲	1:64		$20
❑			
❑			
❑			
❑			

Note: *This is a model of Earnhardt's 1990 car.*

How Many: | Total Value:

Page Totals:	How Many	Total Value

48

Goodwrench

	Scale	LE	Value
❑ Winner's Circle Lifetime Series	1:64		$8

	Scale	LE	Value
❑			
❑			
❑			
❑			

▲ *Pictured car is the 1991 release.*

***Note:** This is a model of Earnhardt's 1991 car.*

How Many: **Total Value:**

49

Goodwrench

	Scale	LE	Value
❑ Winner's Circle Silver Series ▲	1:64		$20

	Scale	LE	Value
❑			
❑			
❑			
❑			

***Note:** This is a model of Earnhardt's 1991 car.*

How Many: **Total Value:**

50

Goodwrench

	Scale	LE	Value
❑ Winner's Circle Lifetime Series ▲	1:64		$8

	Scale	LE	Value
❑			
❑			
❑			
❑			

***Note:** This is a model of Earnhardt's 1993 car.*

How Many: **Total Value:**

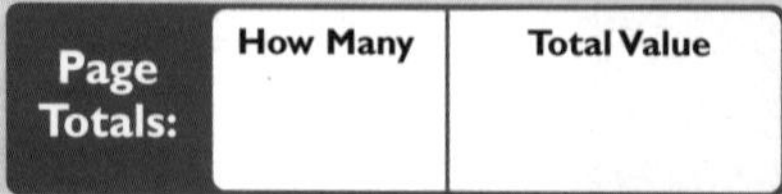

51

Goodwrench

	Scale	LE	Value
❑ Winner's Circle Silver Series ▲	1:64		$18

	Scale	LE	Value
❑			
❑			
❑			
❑			

Note: *This is a model of Earnhardt's 1993 car.*

How Many: **Total Value:**

52

Goodwrench

	Scale	LE	Value
❑ Winner's Circle Lifetime Series	1:64		$8

	Scale	LE	Value
❑			
❑			
❑			
❑			

▲ *Pictured car is the 1994 release.*

Note: *This is a model of Earnhardt's 1994 car.*

How Many: **Total Value:**

53

Goodwrench

	Scale	LE	Value
❑ Winner's Circle Silver Series ▲	1:64		$9

	Scale	LE	Value
❑			
❑			
❑			
❑			

Note: *Earnhardt drove this car in 1994.*

How Many: **Total Value:**

54

Goodwrench

	Scale	LE	Value
❑ Action/RCCA ▲	1:24		$350
❑ Action/RCCA	1:64		N/E

	Scale	LE	Value
❑			
❑			
❑			
❑			

Note: *This is a model of Earnhardt's 1997 car. It is commonly referred to by collectors as the "crash car."*

How Many: **Total Value:**

Page Totals:	How Many	Total Value

55

Goodwrench Plus

	Scale	LE	Value
❑ Action (Daytona 500)	1:18		$105
❑ Action ▲	1:24		$74
❑ Action (Daytona 500)	1:24		$75
❑ Action (Daytona 500)	1:32		$48
❑ Action	1:64		$14
❑ Action (Daytona 500)	1:64		$19
❑ Action (hood open)	1:64		$13
❑ Action/RCCA	1:64		$25
❑ Action/RCCA Elite	1:24		$125
❑ Action/RCCA Elite (Daytona 500)	1:24		$150
❑ Revell Club (Daytona 500)	1:18		$150
❑ Revell Club	1:24		$140
❑ Revell Club (Daytona 500)	1:24		$70
❑ Revell Collection	1:18		$120
❑ Revell Collection	1:24		$65
❑ Revell Collection (Brickyard 400)	1:24		$65
❑ Revell Collection (Daytona 500)	1:24		$70
❑ Revell Collection	1:43		$40
❑ Revell Collection	1:64		$16
❑ Revell Collection (Brickyard 400)	1:64		$13
❑ Revell Select	1:24		$40
❑ Revell Select (Daytona 500)	1:24		$40
❑ Winner's Circle	1:24		N/E
❑ Winner's Circle (Daytona 500)	1:24		N/E
❑ Winner's Circle (Daytona 500)	1:43		$15
❑ Winner's Circle (Daytona 500)	1:64		N/E
❑ Winner's Circle (Toys 'R Us)	1:64		$9
❑ Winner's Circle Lifetime Series	1:64		$8
❑ Winner's Circle Lifetime Series (Daytona 500)	1:64		$8
❑ Winner's Circle Preview	1:24		N/E
❑ Winner's Circle Preview	1:64		$8
❑			
❑			

How Many: Total Value:

56

Goodwrench Plus

	Scale	LE	Value
❑ Action ▲	1:24		N/E
❑ Action/RCCA Elite	1:24		$1,650
❑ Action/RCCA Elite (Canadian)	1:24		$900
❑			
❑			
❑			
❑			

How Many: Total Value:

57

Mike Curb

	Scale	LE	Value
❑ Winner's Circle Lifetime Series ▲	1:64		$34
❑			
❑			
❑			
❑			

Note: *This is a model of Earnhardt's 1980 car.*

How Many: Total Value:

Page Totals:	How Many	Total Value

58

Mike Curb

	Scale	LE	Value
❑ Winner's Circle Silver Series ▲	1:64		$16
❑			
❑			
❑			
❑			

Note: This is a model of Earnhardt's 1980 car.

How Many: Total Value:

59

Olympics

	Scale	LE	Value
❑ Winner's Circle Lifetime Series	1:64		$13
❑			
❑			
❑			
❑			

▲ *Pictured car is the 1996 release.*

Note: This is a model of Earnhardt's 1996 car.

How Many: Total Value:

60

RPM

	Scale	LE	Value
❑ Action	1:24		$64
❑ Action ▲	1:64		$15
❑ Action/RCCA	1:64		$14
❑ Action/RCCA Elite	1:24		$120
❑			
❑			
❑			
❑			

Note: This is a model of Earnhardt's 1975 RPM car.

How Many: Total Value:

61

Wheaties

	Scale	LE	Value
❑ Action	1:18		$120
❑			
❑			
❑			
❑			
❑			

▲ *Pictured car is the 1997 release.*

Note: This is a model of Earnhardt's 1997 car.

How Many: Total Value:

Page Totals:	How Many	Total Value

62

Winston Silver Select

	Scale	LE	Value
❑ Action	1:18		$125
❑ Action	1:32		$70

	Scale	LE	Value
❑ Action/RCCA Elite	1:24		$270
❑ Winner's Circle	1:24		$38
❑			
❑			
❑			
❑			

▲ *Pictured car is the 1995 release.*

Note: *This is a model of the Winston Silver Select car that Earnhardt drove in 1995.*

How Many: **Total Value:**

63

PHOTO UNAVAILABLE

Wrangler

	Scale	LE	Value
❑ Winner's Circle Lifetime Series	1:64		$8

	Scale	LE	Value
❑			
❑			
❑			
❑			

Note: *This is a model of Earnhardt's 1981 Wrangler.*

How Many: **Total Value:**

64

Wrangler

	Scale	LE	Value
❑ Winner's Circle Lifetime Series	1:64		$7

	Scale	LE	Value
❑			
❑			
❑			
❑			

▲ *Pictured car is the 1996 release.*

Note: *This is a model of Earnhardt's 1982 car.*

How Many: **Total Value:**

65

Wrangler

	Scale	LE	Value
❑ Winner's Circle Lifetime Series	1:64		$10

	Scale	LE	Value
❑			
❑			
❑			
❑			

▲ *Pictured car is the 1995 release.*

Note: *This is a model of Earnhardt's 1985 car.*

How Many: **Total Value:**

Page Totals:	How Many	Total Value

66

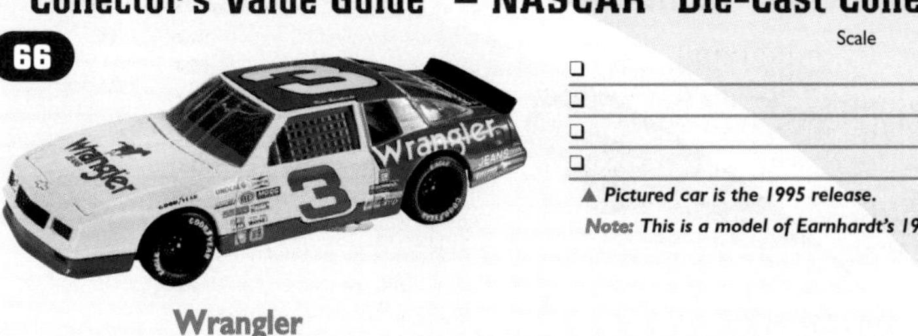

	Scale	LE	Value
❑			
❑			
❑			
❑			

▲ *Pictured car is the 1995 release.*

***Note:** This is a model of Earnhardt's 1987 car.*

Wrangler

	Scale	LE	Value
❑ Winner's Circle Lifetime Series	1:64		$12

How Many: Total Value:

67

	Scale	LE	Value
❑			
❑			
❑			
❑			

***Note:** This is a model of Earnhardt's 1987 car.*

Wrangler

	Scale	LE	Value
❑ Winner's Circle Silver Series ▲	1:64		N/E

How Many: Total Value:

1999 Releases

68

	Scale	LE	Value
❑ Action/RCCA	1:64		$22
❑ Action/RCCA Elite	1:24		$135
❑ Winner's Circle Lifetime Series	1:64		$9
❑			
❑			
❑			

***Note:** This is a model of Earnhardt's 1976 Army car.*

Army

	Scale	LE	Value
❑ Action ▲	1:24		$68
❑ Action	1:64		$15

How Many: Total Value:

69

	Scale	LE	Value
❑			
❑			
❑			
❑			

***Note:** This is a model of Earnhardt's 1979 car.*

Crane Cams

	Scale	LE	Value
❑ Winner's Circle Lifetime Series ▲	1:64		$10

How Many: Total Value:

Page Totals:	How Many	Total Value

70

Goodwrench

	Scale	LE	Value
❑ Winner's Circle Lifetime Series (Daytona 500)	1:64		$7

	Scale	LE	Value
❑			
❑			
❑			
❑			

▲ *Pictured car is the 1995 release.*

Note: *This car is a model of Earnhardt's 1988 car.*

How Many: Total Value:

71

Goodwrench

	Scale	LE	Value
❑ Winner's Circle Lifetime Series ▲	1:64		$7

	Scale	LE	Value
❑			
❑			
❑			
❑			

Note: *This is a model of Earnhardt's 1989 car.*

How Many: Total Value:

72

Goodwrench

	Scale	LE	Value
❑ Winner's Circle 25th Anniversary	1:43		$18

	Scale	LE	Value
❑			
❑			
❑			
❑			

▲ *Pictured car is part of a collector's set.*

Note: *This is a model of Earnhardt's 1990 car.*

How Many: Total Value:

73

Goodwrench

	Scale	LE	Value
❑ Winner's Circle 25th Anniversary Series	1:43		N/E

	Scale	LE	Value
❑			
❑			
❑			
❑			

▲ *Pictured car is the 1998 release.*

Note: *This is a model of Earnhardt's 1993 car.*

How Many: Total Value:

Page Totals:	How Many	Total Value

74

	Scale	LE	Value
❑			
❑			
❑			
❑			

▲ *Pictured car is the 1995 release.*

Note: *This is a model of Earnhardt's 1995 car.*

Goodwrench

	Scale	LE	Value
❑ Winner's Circle Lifetime Series (Brickyard 400)	1:64		$8

How Many: **Total Value:**

75

Goodwrench Plus

	Scale	LE	Value
❑ Action	1:18		$85
❑ Action (25th Anniversary)	1:18		$90
❑ Action	1:24		$65
❑ Action (25th Anniversary)	1:24		$60
❑ Action (Last Lap)	1:24		$85
❑ Action (25th Anniversary)	1:64		$15
❑ Action (Last Lap)	1:64		$16
❑ Action/RCCA	1:64		$20
❑ Action/RCCA (25th Anniversary)	1:64		$25
❑ Action/RCCA (Last Lap)	1:64		$35
❑ Action/RCCA Elite ▲	1:24		$155
❑ Action/RCCA Elite (25th Anniversary)	1:24		$140
❑ Action/RCCA Elite (Last Lap)	1:24		$180
❑ Revell Club	1:18		$135
❑ Revell Club (25th Anniversary)	1:18		$120
❑ Revell Club	1:24		$110
❑ Revell Club (25th Anniversary)	1:24		$70
❑ Revell Collection	1:18		$100
❑ Revell Collection (25th Anniversary)	1:18		$75
❑ Revell Collection	1:24		$65
❑ Revell Collection (25th Anniversary)	1:24		$60
❑ Revell Collection	1:43		$30
❑ Revell Collection	1:64		$12
❑ Revell Collection (25th Anniversary)	1:64		$15
❑ Winner's Circle	1:43		N/E
❑ Winner's Circle Lifetime Series	1:64		$8
❑ Winner's Circle Pro Series	1:64		N/E
❑ Winner's Circle Speedweeks	1:43		$11
❑ Winner's Circle Speedweeks	1:64		$6
❑ Winner's Circle Tech Series	1:64		$12
❑ Winner's Circle Tech Series (Select)	1:64		N/E
❑			

How Many: **Total Value:**

76

Goodwrench Plus

	Scale	LE	Value
❑ Winner's Circle (Wal-Mart Exclusive)	1:43		N/E
❑ Winner's Circle ▲	1:64		$24
❑			
❑			
❑			
❑			

How Many: **Total Value:**

Page Totals:	How Many	Total Value

77

Goodwrench Plus

	Scale	LE	Value
❑ Action	1:18		$95
❑ Action ▲	1:24		$55
❑ Action (Brickyard 400, QVC Exclusive)	1:32		N/E
❑ Action	1:64		$12
❑ Revell Collection	1:24		$50
❑			
❑			
❑			
❑			

How Many:	Total Value:

78

Hy-Gain

	Scale	LE	Value
❑ Action ▲	1:24		$68
❑ Action	1:64		$15
❑ Action/RCCA	1:64		$29
❑ Action/RCCA Elite	1:24		$155
❑ Winner's Circle Lifetime Series	1:64		$6
❑			
❑			
❑			
❑			

***Note:** This is a model of Earnhardt's 1976 car.*

How Many:	Total Value:

79

Mike Curb Wrangler

	Scale	LE	Value
❑ Winner's Circle Lifetime Series ▲	1:64		$10
❑			
❑			
❑			
❑			

***Note:** Earnhardt drove the Mike Curb Wrangler in 1980.*

How Many:	Total Value:

Page Totals:	How Many	Total Value

80

Olympics

	Scale	LE	Value
❑ Winner's Circle	1:43		$17
❑			

	Scale	LE	Value
❑			
❑			
❑			
❑			

▲ *Pictured car is the 1996 release.*

***Note:** This is a model of Earnhardt's 1996 Olympics paint scheme.*

How Many: **Total Value:**

81

Wrangler

	Scale	LE	Value
❑ Winner's Circle Lifetime Series (Talladega)	1:64		$10

	Scale	LE	Value
❑			
❑			
❑			
❑			

▲ *Pictured car is part of a collector's set.*

***Note:** This is a model of Earnhardt's 1984 Wrangler.*

How Many: **Total Value:**

82

Wrangler

	Scale	LE	Value
❑ Winner's Circle Lifetime Series	1:64		N/E

	Scale	LE	Value
❑			
❑			
❑			
❑			

▲ *Pictured car is part of a collector's set.*

***Note:** This is a model of Earnhardt's 1986 Wrangler.*

How Many: **Total Value:**

Dale Earnhardt® – 1999

83

Wrangler

	Scale	LE	Value
❑ Winner's Circle Silver Series ▲	1:64		$13

	Scale	LE	Value
❑			
❑			
❑			
❑			

Note: This is a model of Earnhardt's 1986 car.

How Many: Total Value:

84

Wrangler

	Scale	LE	Value
❑ Winner's Circle 25th Anniversary Series	1:64		$10

	Scale	LE	Value
❑ Winner's Circle Lifetime Series	1:64		$9
❑			
❑			
❑			
❑			

▲ *Pictured car is the 1995 release.*

Note: This is a model of Earnhardt's 1987 car.

How Many: Total Value:

85

Wrangler

	Scale	LE	Value
❑ Action	1:18		$100
❑ Action ▲	1:24		$70
❑ Action	1:64		$16
❑ Action/RCCA	1:32		$54
❑ Action/RCCA	1:64		$35
❑ Action/RCCA Elite	1:24		$200
❑ Revell Club	1:18		$120
❑ Revell Club	1:24		$120
❑ Revell Collection	1:18		$100
❑ Revell Collection	1:24		$60
❑ Revell Collection	1:43		$38
❑ Revell Collection	1:64		$16
❑ Winner's Circle	1:43		$12
❑ Winner's Circle Lifetime Series	1:64		$7
❑			

	Scale	LE	Value
❑			
❑			
❑			
❑			

How Many: Total Value:

Page Totals:	How Many	Total Value

2000 Releases

86

Goodwrench Plus

	Scale	LE	Value
❑ Action ▲	1:24		$60
❑ Action	1:64		$12
❑ Action/RCCA	1:64		$16
❑ Action/RCCA Elite	1:24		$115
❑ Revell Club	1:24		$30
❑ Revell Collection	1:24		$50
❑ Revell Collection	1:64		$13
❑ Winner's Circle	1:24		N/E
❑ Winner's Circle	1:64		$6
❑ Winner's Circle Deluxe (white outlining)	1:64		$6
❑ Winner's Circle Deluxe with emblem	1:64		$10
❑ Winner's Circle Sneak Preview	1:24		$16
❑ Winner's Circle Sneak Preview	1:64		$5
❑ Winner's Circle Speedweeks	1:64		$5
❑			
❑			
❑			
❑			

How Many: Total Value:

87

Goodwrench Plus (gold)

	Scale	LE	Value
❑ Action (QVC Exclusive)	1:24		$200
❑			
❑			
❑			
❑			
❑			

How Many: Total Value:

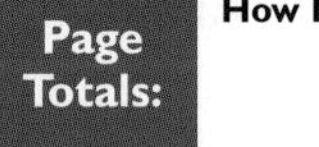

Page Totals:	How Many	Total Value

COLLECTOR'S VALUE GUIDE™

88

Goodwrench Plus

	Scale	LE	Value
❑ Action/RCCA ▲	1:24		N/E
❑			

	Scale	LE	Value
❑			
❑			
❑			
❑			

How Many: Total Value:

89

Goodwrench Plus

	Scale	LE	Value
❑ Action/RCCA Elite ▲	1:24		$185
❑ Revell Collection	1:24		$200

	Scale	LE	Value
❑			
❑			
❑			
❑			

How Many: Total Value:

90

Hy-Gain

	Scale	LE	Value
❑ Winner's Circle Lifetime Series	1:64		$6

	Scale	LE	Value
❑			
❑			
❑			
❑			

▲ *Pictured car is the 1999 release.*

Note: *This is a model of Earnhardt's 1976 Hy-Gain.*

How Many: Total Value:

Page Totals:	How Many	Total Value

91

Peter Max

	Scale	LE	Value
❑ Action	1:18		$90
❑ Action ▲	1:24		$65

	Scale	LE	Value
❑ Action	1:64		$25
❑ Action/RCCA	1:64		$38
❑ Action/RCCA Elite	1:24		$140
❑ Revell Collection	1:24		$60
❑ Revell Collection	1:43		$35
❑ Revell Collection	1:64		N/E
❑			
❑			
❑			
❑			

How Many: | Total Value:

92

Peter Max

	Scale	LE	Value
❑ Action (QVC Exclusive) ▲	1:24		$160

	Scale	LE	Value
❑			
❑			
❑			
❑			

How Many: | Total Value:

93

Taz No Bull

	Scale	LE	Value
❑ Action	1:18		$90
❑ Action	1:24		$75

	Scale	LE	Value
❑ Action	1:32		$50
❑ Action	1:64		$20
❑ Action/RCCA	1:64		$22
❑ Action/RCCA Elite	1:24		$140
❑ Revell Club	1:18		$100
❑ Revell Club	1:24		$80
❑ Revell Collection	1:43		$33
❑ Revell Collection ▲	1:64		$15
❑ Winner's Circle	1:24		$18
❑ Winner's Circle Deluxe	1:64		$38
❑			

How Many: | Total Value:

94

Taz No Bull

	Scale	LE	Value
❑ Action (QVC Exclusive) ▲	1:24		$145

	Scale	LE	Value
❑			
❑			
❑			
❑			

How Many: | Total Value:

Page Totals:	How Many	Total Value

95

	Scale	LE	Value
❑			
❑			
❑			
❑			

Taz No Bull

	Scale	LE	Value
❑ Action (QVC Exclusive) ▲	1:24		$220

How Many: | Total Value:

Page Totals:	How Many	Total Value

Future Releases

Check our web site, ***CollectorsQuest.com***, for new Dale Earnhardt product releases and record the information here.

Dale Earnhardt®	Value	How Many	Total Value

Page Totals:	How Many	Total Value

Future Releases

Check our web site, ***CollectorsQuest.com***, for new Dale Earnhardt product releases and record the information here.

Dale Earnhardt®	Value	How Many	Total Value

Page Totals:	How Many	Total Value

Dale Earnhardt Jr.

Dale Earnhardt Jr. hasn't been racing in NASCAR long enough to amass a large number of paint schemes, but those he has had are much in demand. The #8 Budweiser-sponsored car he drives in the Winston Cup Series is a tribute to both his grandfather and his father, who both drove a #8 car in the past. Fans of Earnhardt Jr.'s Busch Series successes, meanwhile, are more familiar with his ACDelco car. Special paint schemes have included Superman and last year's Last Lap Of The Century promotion.

1994 Releases

1

Mom 'N' Pop's

	Scale	LE	Value
❑ Action/RCCA ▲	1:64		$95

	Scale	LE	Value
❑			
❑			
❑			
❑			

How Many: Total Value:

1998 Releases

2

ACDelco

	Scale	LE	Value
❑ Action	1:24		$230
❑ Action (BGN Champ) ▲	1:24		$150
❑ Action	1:32		$70
❑ Action	1:64		$38
❑ Action (BGN Champ)	1:64		$28
❑ Action/RCCA	1:64		$60
❑ Action/RCCA Elite	1:24		$530
❑ Revell Club	1:18		$285
❑ Revell Club	1:24		$240
❑ Revell Collection	1:18		$175
❑ Revell Collection	1:24		$130
❑ Revell Collection	1:64		$47
❑ Revell Select	1:24		$75
❑ Revell Select	1:64		$23
❑ Winner's Circle	1:24		$40
❑ Winner's Circle	1:43		$23
❑ Winner's Circle	1:64		$15
❑ Winner's Circle (BGN Champ)	1:64		$15
❑			
❑			
❑			
❑			

Note: *Earnhardt Jr.'s first Busch victory came on April 4, 1998 at the Texas Motor Speedway.*

How Many: Total Value:

Page Totals:	How Many	Total Value

3

ACDelco

	Scale	LE	Value
❑ Action/RCCA 24K Gold	1:24		N/E
❑ Action/RCCA 24K Gold ▲	1:32		$110

	Scale	LE	Value
❑			
❑			
❑			
❑			

Note: *Dale Earnhardt Jr. won his first Busch Grand National Championship in 1998.*

How Many:	Total Value:

4

Coca-Cola Polar Bear

	Scale	LE	Value
❑ Action	1:24		$70
❑ Action	1:64		$20

	Scale	LE	Value
❑ Action/RCCA	1:64		$38
❑ Action/RCCA Elite	1:24		$200
❑ Revell Club	1:18		$165
❑ Revell Club ▲	1:24		$140
❑ Revell Collection	1:18		$115
❑ Revell Collection	1:24		$85
❑ Revell Collection	1:43		$40
❑ Revell Collection	1:64		$25
❑ Winner's Circle	1:24		N/E
❑ Winner's Circle	1:43		$14
❑			

How Many:	Total Value:

5

Sikkens

	Scale	LE	Value
❑ Action	1:18		$130
❑ Action ▲	1:24		$185

	Scale	LE	Value
❑ Action	1:64		$35
❑ Action/RCCA	1:64		$52
❑ Action/RCCA Elite	1:24		$300
❑			
❑			
❑			
❑			

Note: *"Little E," as Dale Earnhardt Jr. is known, raced against his father for the first time in a Japanese exhibition race in 1998.*

How Many:	Total Value:

6

Wrangler

	Scale	LE	Value
❑ Action ▲	1:24		$230
❑ Action	1:64		$35

	Scale	LE	Value
❑ Revell Collection	1:18		$200
❑ Revell Collection	1:24		$280
❑ Revell Collection	1:43		$80
❑			
❑			
❑			
❑			

Note: *Country singer Clint Black advertised his "Nothin' But The Taillights" tour on the back of Earnhardt Jr.'s race car during the 1998 season.*

How Many:	Total Value:

Page Totals:	How Many	Total Value

1999 Releases

7

ACDelco

	Scale	LE	Value
❑ Action ▲	1:18		$120
❑ Action	1:24		$85
❑ Action (Last Lap)	1:24		$105
❑ Action	1:64		$17
❑ Action (black window)	1:64		$17
❑ Action (Last Lap)	1:64		$26
❑ Action/RCCA	1:64		$35
❑ Action/RCCA (Fan Club)	1:64		N/E
❑ Action/RCCA (Last Lap)	1:64		$40
❑ Action/RCCA Elite	1:24		$220
❑ Action/RCCA Elite (Last Lap)	1:24		$225
❑ Action/RCCA SelectNet	1:64		N/E
❑ Revell Club	1:24		$100
❑ Revell Collection	1:24		$75
❑ Revell Collection	1:43		$37
❑ Revell Collection	1:64		$19
❑ Winner's Circle	1:24		$37
❑ Winner's Circle	1:43		$15
❑ Winner's Circle (Texas)	1:43		N/E
❑ Winner's Circle	1:64		$12
❑ Winner's Circle Tech Series	1:64		$15
❑			
❑			
❑			
❑			

***Note:** Dale Earnhardt Jr. debuted on the Winston Cup circuit in 1999, a year that saw him run in five events.*

How Many: Total Value:

8

ACDelco

	Scale	LE	Value
❑ Winner's Circle 24K Gold (Target Exclusive) ▲	1:24		N/E
❑ Winner's Circle 24K Gold	1:64		$25
❑			
❑			
❑			
❑			

***Note:** In 1999, Dale Earnhardt Jr. won his second Busch Grand National Championship, making him the fourth driver in history to win the award in consecutive years.*

How Many: Total Value:

Page Totals:	How Many	Total Value

9

Budweiser

	Scale	LE	Value
❑ Action	1:18		$140
❑ Action	1:24		$122
❑ Action (Atlanta)	1:24		$100
❑ Action (Michigan)	1:24		$100
❑ Action (New Hampshire)	1:24		$100
❑ Action (Richmond)	1:24		$100
❑ Action	1:32		$60
❑ Action	1:64		$23
❑ Action (Atlanta)	1:64		$20
❑ Action (Michigan)	1:64		$20
❑ Action (New Hampshire)	1:64		$20
❑ Action (Richmond)	1:64		$20
❑ Action/RCCA	1:64		$40
❑ Action/RCCA (Atlanta)	1:64		$32
❑ Action/RCCA (Michigan)	1:64		$32
❑ Action/RCCA (New Hampshire)	1:64		$32
❑ Action/RCCA (Richmond)	1:64		$32
❑ Action/RCCA Elite	1:24		$250
❑ Action/RCCA Elite (Atlanta)	1:24		$200
❑ Action/RCCA Elite (Michigan)	1:24		$200
❑ Action/RCCA Elite (New Hampshire)	1:24		$200
❑ Action/RCCA Elite (Richmond)	1:24		$200
❑ Action/RCCA Elite SelectNet ▲	1:24		N/E
❑ Revell Club	1:24		$165
❑ Revell Collection	1:18		$128
❑ Revell Collection	1:24		$85
❑ Revell Collection	1:43		$48
❑ Revell Collection	1:64		$23
❑			
❑			
❑			
❑			

Note: *In 1999, Earnhardt Jr. was named the NASCAR Winston Cup Scene Most Popular Driver for the Busch Series.*

How Many:	Total Value:

10

Coca-Cola Polar Bear

	Scale	LE	Value
❑ Action	1:18		$122
❑ Winner's Circle	1:24		$24
❑ Winner's Circle ▲	1:64		$15
❑			
❑			
❑			
❑			

How Many:	Total Value:

Page Totals:	How Many	Total Value

11

Gargoyles

	Scale	LE	Value
❑ Action	1:24		$120
❑ Action	1:32		$55

	Scale	LE	Value
❑ Action	1:64		$25
❑ Action/RCCA	1:64		$44
❑ Action/RCCA Elite	1:24		$190
❑ Revell Club	1:18		$155
❑ Revell Club	1:24		$125
❑ Revell Collection ▲	1:18		$110
❑ Revell Collection	1:24		$83
❑ Revell Collection	1:64		$24
❑ Winner's Circle	1:43		N/E
❑ Winner's Circle	1:64		$12
❑			

How Many: | Total Value:

12

Mom 'N' Pop's

	Scale	LE	Value
❑ Action ▲	1:24		$50
❑ Action	1:64		$22

	Scale	LE	Value
❑ Action/RCCA Elite	1:24		$170
❑ Revell Collection	1:24		$75
❑ Revell Collection	1:64		$22
❑			
❑			
❑			
❑			

Note: *In 1999, Dale Earnhardt Jr. set a Busch Series record with winnings of nearly $1.7 million.*

How Many: | Total Value:

13

Sikkens

	Scale	LE	Value
❑ Action ▲	1:18		$75
❑ Revell Club	1:18		$170

	Scale	LE	Value
❑ Revell Club	1:24		$120
❑ Revell Collection	1:18		$150
❑ Revell Collection	1:24		$80
❑ Revell Collection	1:64		$22
❑ Winner's Circle	1:43		N/E
❑ Winner's Circle	1:64		$11
❑			
❑			
❑			

Note: *Dale Earnhardt, Inc. owns the cars that Dale Jr. races on the Winston Cup circuit.*

How Many: | Total Value:

14

Sikkens

	Scale	LE	Value
❑ Action	1:18		$130
❑ Action	1:24		$115

	Scale	LE	Value
❑ Action	1:64		$24
❑ Action/RCCA	1:64		$33
❑ Action/RCCA Elite ▲	1:24		$225
❑ Action/RCCA Elite SelectNet	1:24		N/E
❑ Action/RCCA SelectNet	1:64		N/E
❑ Revell Club	1:18		$150
❑ Revell Club	1:24		$120
❑ Revell Collection	1:18		$112
❑ Revell Collection	1:24		$75
❑ Revell Collection	1:64		$20
❑			

How Many: | Total Value:

Page Totals:	How Many	Total Value

15

Superman

	Scale	LE	Value
❑ Action	1:18		$130
❑ Action ▲	1:24		$96
❑ Action	1:64		$23
❑ Action/RCCA Elite	1:24		$225
❑ Action/RCCA	1:64		$37
❑ Revell Club	1:18		$50
❑ Revell Club	1:24		$130
❑ Revell Collection	1:18		$105
❑ Revell Collection	1:24		$75
❑ Revell Collection	1:43		$35
❑ Revell Collection	1:64		$22
❑			

How Many: Total Value:

16

Wrangler

	Scale	LE	Value
❑ Action ▲	1:18		$140
❑ Action/RCCA	1:64		$42
❑ Action/RCCA Elite	1:24		$205
❑ Revell Collection	1:24		N/E
❑ Winner's Circle	1:43		N/E
❑ Winner's Circle	1:64		$13
❑			
❑			
❑			
❑			

How Many: Total Value:

2000 Releases

17

Budweiser

	Scale	LE	Value
❑ Action	1:18		$75
❑ Action	1:24		$115
❑ Action (Brickyard 400)	1:24		$100
❑ Action	1:64		$18
❑ Action/RCCA	1:64		$35
❑ Action/RCCA Elite	1:24		$190
❑ Revell Club	1:18		$155
❑ Revell Club	1:24		$145
❑ Revell Collection ▲	1:24		$80
❑ Revell Collection	1:64		$20
❑ Winner's Circle Deluxe	1:64		N/E
❑			

How Many: Total Value:

18

Budweiser

	Scale	LE	Value
❑ Action 24K Gold ▲	1:24		$200
❑			
❑			
❑			
❑			
❑			

How Many: Total Value:

Page Totals:	How Many	Total Value

19

Budweiser

	Scale	LE	Value
❑ Action/RCCA Elite ▲	1:24		$240
❑ Revell Collection	1:24		$175

	Scale	LE	Value
❑			
❑			
❑			
❑			

Note: *Dale Earnhardt Jr.'s crew chief is Tony Eury.*

How Many: **Total Value:**

20

2000 Olympics

	Scale	LE	Value
❑ Action ▲	1:24		N/E
❑ Action Total Concept	1:64		N/E

	Scale	LE	Value
❑ Action/RCCA	1:24		N/E
❑ Action/RCCA	1:64		N/E
❑ Action/RCCA Elite	1:24		N/E
❑ Action/RCCA Total View	1:64		N/E
❑ Revell Club	1:24		N/E
❑ Revell Collection	1:24		N/E
❑ Revell Collection	1:64		N/E
❑			
❑			
❑			

How Many: **Total Value:**

Future Releases

Check our web site, ***CollectorsQuest.com***, for new Dale Earnhardt Jr. product releases and record the information here.

Dale Earnhardt Jr.	Value	How Many	Total Value

Page Totals:	How Many	Total Value

Jeff Gordon®

Jeff Gordon's chief sponsor is DuPont, whose special ChromaLusion paint makes his cars especially popular among collectors. Gordon has also run a variety of promotional paint schemes, including the Jurassic Park scheme he ran in 1997 to promote the movie *The Lost World* and the 1999 Star Wars scheme promoting the movie *Episode One: The Phantom Menace*. Meanwhile, models of the Peanuts-themed paint scheme which he ran in 2000 to honor Charles Schulz are certain to become popular collectibles.

1992 Releases

1

Baby Ruth

	Scale	LE	Value
❑ Action/RCCA	1:64		$80
❑ Ertl	1:18		$140
❑ Matchbox/White Rose Super Stars (orange)	1:64		$42
❑ Matchbox/White Rose Super Stars (red)	1:64		$35
❑ Racing Champions	1:24		$830
❑ Racing Champions	1:43		$100
❑ Racing Champions	1:64		$115
❑ Revell	1:24		$500

▲ *Pictured car is the 1998 release.*

How Many: | Total Value:

1993 Releases

2

DuPont

	Scale	LE	Value
❑ Matchbox/White Rose Super Stars	1:64		$16
❑ Matchbox/White Rose Super Stars (Rookie Of The Year)	1:64		$18
❑ Racing Champions ▲	1:24		$150
❑ Racing Champions	1:43		$32
❑ Racing Champions	1:64		$48
❑ Racing Champions PVC Box	1:64		$45
❑ Racing Champions PVC Box (Daytona 500)	1:64		$45
❑ Racing Champions Premier	1:43		$75
❑ Racing Champions Premier	1:64		$100
❑ Racing Champions Premier (1st Pole)	1:64		N/E
❑ Racing Champions Premier (Rookie Of The Year)	1:64		$100
❑			
❑			
❑			
❑			

***Note:** Gordon's two second-place finishes helped him capture Winston Cup Rookie Of The Year honors in 1993.*

How Many: | Total Value:

Page Totals:	How Many	Total Value

1994 Releases

3

DuPont

	Scale	LE	Value
❑ Action	1:64		$50
❑ Action/RCCA	1:64		$86
❑ Matchbox/White Rose Super Stars	1:64		$15
❑ Racing Champions (Brickyard 400)	1:24		$110
❑ Racing Champions (Coca-Cola 600)	1:24		$155
❑ Racing Champions (with Snickers)	1:24		$90
❑ Racing Champions (without Snickers)	1:24		$135
❑ Racing Champions	1:43		$60
❑ Racing Champions	1:64		$48
❑ Racing Champions (Brickyard 400)	1:64		$40
❑ Racing Champions (Coca-Cola 600)	1:64		$95
❑ Racing Champions (yellow box)	1:64		$45
❑ Racing Champions Premier	1:43		$45
❑ Racing Champions Premier (Brickyard 400)	1:43		$90
❑ Racing Champions Premier	1:64		$85
❑ Racing Champions Premier (Brickyard 400)	1:64		$125
❑ Racing Champions PVC Box (Fan Club)	1:64		N/E
❑ Racing Champions To The MAXX	1:64		$40
❑ Revell ▲	1:24		$115
❑			
❑			
❑			
❑			

Note: Gordon's first Winston Cup win came driving this car in the Coca-Cola 600 on May 29, 1994.

How Many:	Total Value:

1995 Releases

4

DuPont

	Scale	LE	Value
❑ Action	1:64		$23
❑ Action/RCCA ▲	1:24		$200
❑ Action/RCCA	1:64		$40
❑ Ertl (Buck Fever)	1:18		$135
❑ Ertl (by GMP)	1:18		$140
❑ Matchbox/White Rose Super Stars	1:64		$13
❑ Racing Champions	1:18		$90
❑ Racing Champions (Winston Cup Champ)	1:18		$115
❑ Racing Champions	1:24		$80
❑ Racing Champions (Winston Cup Champ)	1:24		$100
❑ Racing Champions	1:64		$34
❑ Racing Champions Matched Serial Numbers	1:64		$36
❑ Racing Champions Premier (Winston Cup Champ)	1:24		$110
❑ Racing Champions Premier	1:64		$45
❑ Racing Champions Premier (Winston Cup Champ)	1:64		$17
❑ Racing Champions PVC Box (Fan Club)	1:64		N/E
❑ Racing Champions Signature Driver Series	1:18		$95
❑ Racing Champions Signature Driver Series	1:24		$86
❑ Racing Champions Signature Driver Series (hood open)	1:24		$98
❑ Racing Champions Signature Driver Series	1:64		$40
❑ Racing Champions To The MAXX	1:64		$22
❑ Revell	1:24		$78
❑			
❑			
❑			
❑			

How Many:	Total Value:

Page Totals:	How Many	Total Value

1996 Releases

5

Baby Ruth

	Scale	LE	Value
❑ Ertl	1:18		$140

	Scale	LE	Value
❑			
❑			
❑			
❑			

▲ *Pictured car is the 1998 release.*

Note: *This is the car that Jeff Gordon drove in 1992.*

How Many: **Total Value:**

6

DuPont

	Scale	LE	Value
❑ Action	1:64		$20
❑ Action/RCCA ▲	1:24		$120
❑ Action/RCCA	1:64		$50
❑ Matchbox/White Rose Super Stars	1:64		$10
❑ Matchbox/White Rose Super Star Awards	1:64		$40
❑ Racing Champions	1:24		$80
❑ Racing Champions	1:64		$35
❑ Racing Champions	1:144		$35
❑ Racing Champions Premier	1:64		$23
❑ Racing Champions Preview	1:24		$68
❑ Racing Champions Preview	1:64		$3
❑ Racing Champions Promo (Unocal pack)	1:64		$42
❑ Racing Champions PVC Box (Fan Club)	1:64		N/E

	Scale	LE	Value
❑ Revell	1:24		$55
❑ Revell	1:64		$14
❑ Revell Collection	1:24		$75
❑			
❑			
❑			
❑			

Note: *Gordon drove his 1996 DuPont Monte Carlo to ten wins in the 1996 season.*

How Many: **Total Value:**

7

DuPont

	Scale	LE	Value
❑ Racing Champions Chrome Chase	1:64		$275

	Scale	LE	Value
❑			
❑			
❑			
❑			

How Many: **Total Value:**

1997 Releases

8

Baby Ruth

	Scale	LE	Value
❑ Winner's Circle Lifetime Series	1:64		$17

	Scale	LE	Value
❑			
❑			
❑			
❑			

▲ *Pictured car is the 1998 release.*

Note: *Gordon drove this car in 1992.*

How Many: **Total Value:**

9

Carolina Ford

	Scale	LE	Value
❑ Winner's Circle	1:64		$16
❑			

	Scale	LE	Value
❑			
❑			
❑			
❑			

▲ *Pictured car is the 1999 release.*

Note: *Gordon won the Busch Rookie Of The Year title in 1991 after a strong season driving this car.*

How Many: **Total Value:**

10

Chroma Premier

	Scale	LE	Value
❑ Action	1:24		$190
❑ Action	1:64		$33

	Scale	LE	Value
❑ Action/RCCA	1:24		$300
❑ Action/RCCA	1:64		$60
❑ Action/RCCA Elite ▲	1:24		$420
❑ Winner's Circle	1:24		$42
❑ Winner's Circle Lifetime Series	1:64		$24
❑			
❑			
❑			
❑			

How Many: **Total Value:**

11

DuPont

	Scale	LE	Value
❑ Winner's Circle Lifetime Series	1:64		$17

	Scale	LE	Value
❑			
❑			
❑			
❑			

▲ *Pictured car is the 1993 release.*

Note: *Gordon drove this car in 1993.*

How Many: **Total Value:**

Page Totals:	How Many	Total Value

12

DuPont

	Scale	LE	Value
❑ Action ▲	1:24		$82
❑ Action (Brickyard 400)	1:24		$72
❑ Action (Brickyard 400)	1:64		$17
❑ Action (Million Dollar Date)	1:64		$22
❑ Action (Million Dollar Date, black window)	1:64		$22
❑ Action/RCCA (Million Dollar Date)	1:24		$140
❑ Action/RCCA	1:64		$35
❑ Action/RCCA (Million Dollar Date)	1:64		$35
❑ Action/RCCA Elite	1:24		$355
❑ Action/RCCA Elite (Million Dollar Date)	1:24		$200
❑ Action/ RCCA Elite	1:64		$24
❑ Racing Champions	1:24		$75
❑ Racing Champions	1:64		$25
❑ Racing Champions	1:144		$22
❑ Racing Champions Premier Preview	1:64		$25
❑ Racing Champions Preview	1:24		$65
❑ Racing Champions Preview	1:64		$18
❑ Racing Champions PVC Box (Fan Club)	1:64		N/E
❑ Winner's Circle	1:24		$35
❑ Winner's Circle	1:64		$15
❑ Winner's Circle Lifetime Series (Million Dollar Date)	1:24		$40
❑ Winner's Circle Lifetime Series (Million Dollar Date)	1:64		$16
❑			
❑			
❑			
❑			

How Many: | Total Value:

13

Jurassic Park

	Scale	LE	Value
❑ Action/RCCA	1:24		$188
❑ Action/RCCA	1:64		$50
❑ Action/RCCA Elite ▲	1:24		$325
❑ Winner's Circle	1:24		$52
❑ Winner's Circle Lifetime Series	1:64		$22
❑			
❑			
❑			
❑			

How Many: | Total Value:

Page Totals:	How Many	Total Value

1998 Releases

14

Baby Ruth

	Scale	LE	Value
❑ Action	1:24		$75
❑ Action/RCCA	1:64		$38
❑ Action/RCCA Elite ▲	1:24		$190
❑ Revell Club	1:24		$200
❑			
❑			
❑			
❑			

Note: *Gordon drove this car in 1992.*

How Many:	Total Value:

15

ChromaLusion

	Scale	LE	Value
❑ Action ▲	1:24		$120
❑ Action	1:64		$38
❑ Action/RCCA	1:64		$65
❑ Action/RCCA Elite	1:24		$350
❑ Revell Club	1:18		$215
❑ Revell Club	1:24		$200
❑ Revell Collection	1:18		$150
❑ Revell Collection	1:24		$125
❑ Revell Collection	1:43		$60
❑ Revell Collection	1:64		$38
❑			
❑			

How Many:	Total Value:

16

PHOTO UNAVAILABLE

DuPont

	Scale	LE	Value
❑ Winner's Circle Lifetime Series	1:64		$14
❑			
❑			
❑			
❑			

Note: *Gordon drove this car in 1994.*

How Many:	Total Value:

Page Totals:	How Many	Total Value

17

DuPont

	Scale	LE	Value
❑ Action	1:24		$82
❑ Action (Brickyard 400)	1:24		$140
❑ Action (No Bull)	1:24		$85
❑ Action	1:64		$18
❑ Action (Brickyard 400)	1:64		$17
❑ Action (No Bull)	1:64		$17
❑ Action/RCCA	1:64		$25
❑ Action/RCCA (Fan Club)	1:64		N/E
❑ Action/RCCA (No Bull)	1:64		$36
❑ Action/RCCA Elite	1:24		$250
❑ Action/RCCA Elite (No Bull)	1:24		$210
❑ Revell Club	1:18		$220
❑ Revell Club	1:24		$215
❑ Revell Collection	1:18		$135
❑ Revell Collection ▲	1:24		$78
❑ Revell Collection (Brickyard 400)	1:24		$90
❑ Revell Collection	1:43		$45
❑ Revell Collection	1:64		$16
❑ Revell Collection (Brickyard 400)	1:64		$16
❑ Revell Select	1:24		$52
❑ Revell Select	1:64		$13
❑ Winner's Circle	1:24		$32
❑ Winner's Circle	1:43		$17
❑ Winner's Circle	1:64		$13
❑ Winner's Circle (Winston Cup Champ)	1:64		$11
❑ Winner's Circle Lifetime Series NASCAR 50th Anniversary (Wal-Mart Exclusive)	1:64		N/E
❑			
❑			
❑			
❑			

Note: Jeff Gordon's 13 wins in 1998 tied the modern record.

How Many: Total Value:

18

DuPont

	Scale	LE	Value
❑ Action/RCCA 24K Gold ▲	1:32		$88
❑			
❑			
❑			
❑			

How Many: Total Value:

1999 Releases

19

Baby Ruth

	Scale	LE	Value
❑ Action	1:64		$17
❑			
❑			
❑			
❑			

▲ Pictured car is the 1998 release.

Note: Gordon drove this car in 1992.

How Many: Total Value:

Page Totals:	How Many	Total Value

COLLECTOR'S VALUE GUIDE™

20

Carolina Ford

	Scale	LE	Value
❑ Action	1:24		$92
❑ Action	1:64		$18
❑ Action/RCCA	1:64		$30
❑ Action/RCCA Elite ▲	1:24		$190
❑ Action/RCCA Elite SelectNet	1:24		N/E
❑			
❑			
❑			
❑			

Note: *Gordon drove this car in 1991.*

How Many: | Total Value:

21

DuPont

	Scale	LE	Value
❑ Winner's Circle Lifetime Series ▲	1:64		N/E
❑			
❑			
❑			
❑			

Note: *Gordon ran this car in his only Winston Cup race in 1992.*

How Many: | Total Value:

22

DuPont

	Scale	LE	Value
❑ Action	1:18		$115
❑ Action	1:24		$75
❑ Action	1:64		$18
❑ Action/RCCA	1:64		$28
❑ Action/RCCA (Fan Club)	1:64		N/E
❑ Action/RCCA Elite	1:24		$190
❑ Revell Club	1:24		$95
❑ Revell Club (Daytona 500)	1:24		$130
❑ Revell Collection	1:18		$115
❑ Revell Collection ▲	1:24		$68
❑ Revell Collection (Daytona 500)	1:24		$80
❑ Revell Collection	1:43		$30
❑ Revell Collection	1:64		$16
❑ Revell Collection (Daytona 500)	1:64		$19
❑ Winner's Circle	1:24		$33
❑ Winner's Circle (Daytona 500)	1:64		$13
❑ Winner's Circle Lifetime Series	1:64		N/E
❑ Winner's Circle Speedweeks	1:64		$12
❑			
❑			
❑			
❑			

Note: *Jeff Gordon had a solid seven-win season in this car.*

How Many: | Total Value:

Page Totals:	How Many	Total Value

23

DuPont

	Scale	LE	Value
❑ Winner's Circle Gold Collection ▲	1:64		$22

	Scale	LE	Value
❑			
❑			
❑			
❑			

How Many: | Total Value:

24

DuPont

	Scale	LE	Value
❑ Action 24K Gold ▲	1:24		$200
❑			

	Scale	LE	Value
❑			
❑			
❑			
❑			

How Many: | Total Value:

25

NASCAR Racers

	Scale	LE	Value
❑ Action	1:18		$120
❑ Action ▲	1:24		$110

	Scale	LE	Value
❑ Action	1:64		$18
❑ Action/RCCA	1:64		$30
❑ Action/RCCA Elite	1:24		$175
❑ Winner's Circle	1:64		N/E
❑			
❑			
❑			
❑			

How Many: | Total Value:

26

Outback Steakhouse

	Scale	LE	Value
❑ Winner's Circle Lifetime Series	1:64		N/E

	Scale	LE	Value
❑			
❑			
❑			
❑			

▲ *Pictured car is the 2000 release.*

Note: *The Outback Steakhouse car was Gordon's first entry into the world of stock car racing. He drove it in 1990, his first year of Busch Series competition.*

How Many: | Total Value:

Page Totals:	How Many	Total Value

27

Pepsi

	Scale	LE	Value
❑ Action ▲	1:18		$140
❑ Action	1:24		$80
❑ Action	1:64		$18
❑ Action/RCCA	1:64		$30
❑ Action/RCCA Elite	1:24		$245
❑ Action/RCCA Elite SelectNet	1:24		N/E
❑ Action/RCCA Elite SelectNet	1:64		N/E
❑ Revell Club	1:18		$145
❑ Revell Club	1:24		$135
❑ Revell Collection	1:18		$140
❑ Revell Collection	1:24		$82
❑ Revell Collection	1:43		$32
❑ Revell Collection	1:64		$18
❑ WInner's Circle	1:24		$32
❑ WInner's Circle	1:43		$18
❑ WInner's Circle	1:64		$10
❑			
❑			
❑			
❑			

Note: *Gordon drove this Pepsi car in his brief return to Busch Series racing.*

How Many: Total Value:

28

Pepsi – Star Wars

	Scale	LE	Value
❑ Action	1:18		$120
❑ Action ▲	1:24		$85
❑ Action	1:64		$18
❑ Action/RCCA	1:64		$30
❑ Action/RCCA Elite	1:24		$215
❑ Revell Club	1:24		$150
❑ Revell Collection	1:18		$128
❑ Revell Collection	1:24		$85
❑ Revell Collection	1:43		$34
❑ Revell Collection	1:64		$18
❑			

Note: *On May 29, 1999, Gordon raced this car at Charlotte's Lowe's Motor Speedway.*

How Many: Total Value:

29

Superman

	Scale	LE	Value
❑ Action	1:18		$135
❑ Action ▲	1:24		$100
❑ Action	1:64		$23
❑ Action/RCCA	1:32		$66
❑ Action/RCCA	1:64		$35
❑ Action/RCCA Elite	1:24		$250
❑ Revell Club	1:18		$185
❑ Revell Club	1:24		$175
❑ Revell Collection	1:24		$100
❑ Revell Collection	1:43		$40
❑ Revell Collection	1:64		$24
❑ Winner's Circle Lifetime Series	1:64		$10

How Many: Total Value:

Page Totals:	How Many	Total Value

2000 Releases

30

DuPont

	Scale	LE	Value
❑ Action	1:18		$85
❑ Action ▲	1:24		$70

	Scale	LE	Value
❑ Action	1:64		$15
❑ Revell Collection	1:64		$16
❑ Winner's Circle Preview	1:24		$32
❑ Winner's Circle Preview	1:43		$14
❑ Winner's Circle Preview	1:64		$10
❑			
❑			

How Many: | Total Value:

31

DuPont

	Scale	LE	Value
❑ Action 24K Gold (QVC Exclusive) ▲	1:24		$185

	Scale	LE	Value
❑			
❑			
❑			
❑			

How Many: | Total Value:

32

DuPont

	Scale	LE	Value
❑ Action ▲	1:18		N/E
❑ Action	1:24		N/E

	Scale	LE	Value
❑ Action	1:64		N/E
❑ Action/RCCA	1:64		N/E
❑ Action/RCCA Elite	1:24		N/E
❑ Action/RCCA TotalView	1:64		N/E
❑ Revell Collection	1:64		N/E
❑			
❑			
❑			
❑			

How Many: | Total Value:

33

DuPont

	Scale	LE	Value
❑ Revell Collection ▲	1:24		$225
❑			

	Scale	LE	Value
❑			
❑			
❑			
❑			

How Many: | Total Value:

Page Totals:	How Many	Total Value

34

NASCAR 2000

	Scale	LE	Value
❑ Action ▲	1:24		$75
❑ Action	1:64		$17
❑ Action/RCCA	1:64		$28
❑ Action/RCCA Elite	1:24		$162
❑ Action/RCCA TotalView	1:64		$30
❑ Revell Club	1:18		$105
❑ Winner's Circle (Kmart Exclusive)	1:64		N/E
❑			
❑			
❑			
❑			

How Many: Total Value:

35

Outback Steakhouse

	Scale	LE	Value
❑ Action/RCCA ▲	1:64		N/E
❑ Action/RCCA Elite	1:24		N/E
❑			
❑			
❑			
❑			

Note: *Gordon drove the Outback Steakhouse car in 1990, his first year of Busch Series competition.*

How Many: Total Value:

36

Peanuts

	Scale	LE	Value
❑ Action	1:18		N/E
❑ Action ▲	1:24		N/E
❑ Action	1:64		N/E
❑ Action/RCCA Elite	1:24		N/E
❑ Action/RCCA TotalView	1:64		N/E
❑ Action Total Concept	1:64		N/E
❑ Revell Collection	1:24		N/E
❑			
❑			
❑			
❑			

Note: *This car commemorates 50 years of the* Peanuts *comic strip.*

How Many: Total Value:

37

Pepsi

	Scale	LE	Value
❑ Action	1:64		$14
❑ Action/RCCA Elite ▲	1:24		$120
❑ Action/RCCA TotalView	1:64		$20
❑ Revell Collection	1:64		$15
❑			
❑			
❑			
❑			

How Many: Total Value:

Page Totals:	How Many	Total Value

Future Releases

Check our web site, ***CollectorsQuest.com***, for new Jeff Gordon product releases and record the information here.

Jeff Gordon®	Value	How Many	Total Value

Page Totals:	How Many	Total Value

Future Releases

Check our web site, ***CollectorsQuest.com***, for new Jeff Gordon product releases and record the information here.

Jeff Gordon®	Value	How Many	Total Value

Page Totals:	How Many	Total Value

Dale Jarrett®

Dale Jarrett has been racing in the Winston Cup series since 1984. His main sponsor is Ford Quality Care. Although Jarrett hasn't run many special paint schemes, the ones he has are very popular. In 1998, Jarrett ran a special scheme promoting the movie *Batman*, which complemented the Joker paint scheme on the car of teammate Kenny Irwin. Another popular Jarrett car is the Thunderbird with which he won the 1996 Daytona 500; this was the first car ever to be displayed in Victory Lane at the Daytona USA amusement park outside the racetrack's gates.

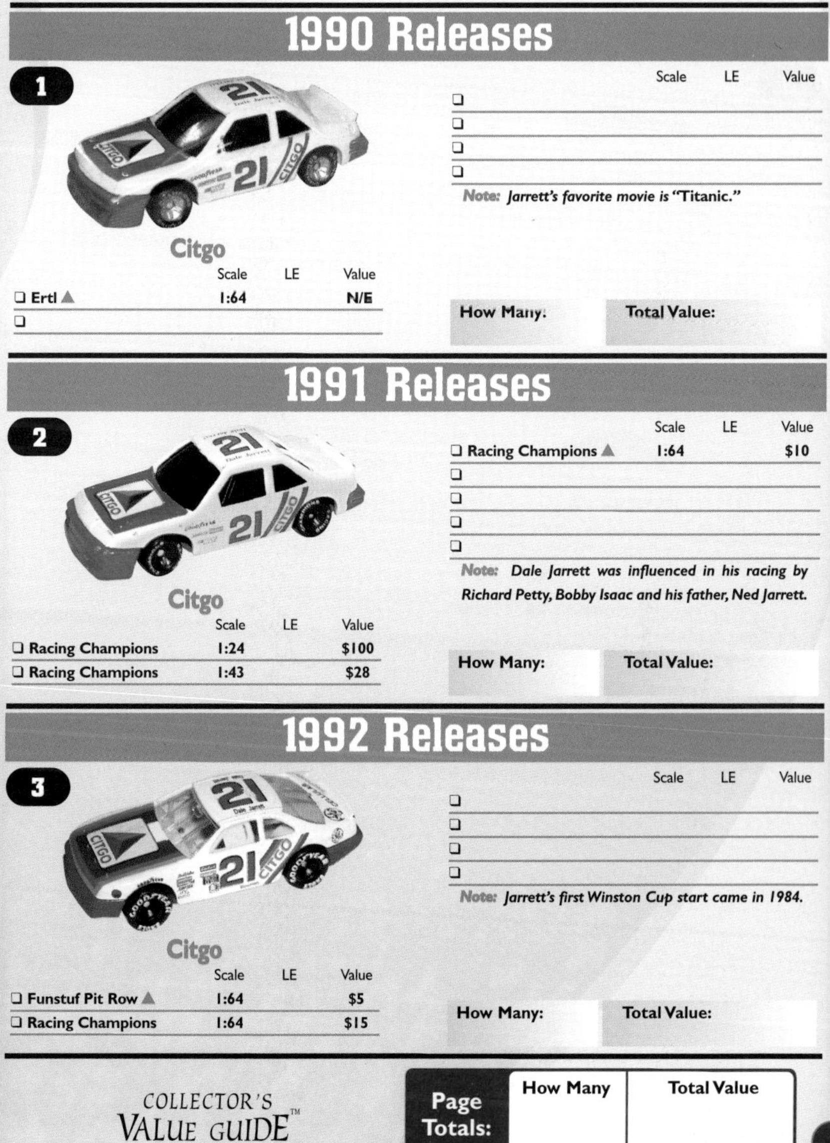

1990 Releases

1

Citgo

	Scale	LE	Value
❑ Ertl ▲	1:64		N/E
❑			

	Scale	LE	Value
❑			
❑			
❑			
❑			

Note: *Jarrett's favorite movie is "Titanic."*

How Many: Total Value:

1991 Releases

2

Citgo

	Scale	LE	Value
❑ Racing Champions	1:24		$100
❑ Racing Champions	1:43		$28

	Scale	LE	Value
❑ Racing Champions ▲	1:64		$10
❑			
❑			
❑			
❑			

Note: *Dale Jarrett was influenced in his racing by Richard Petty, Bobby Isaac and his father, Ned Jarrett.*

How Many: Total Value:

1992 Releases

3

Citgo

	Scale	LE	Value
❑ Funstuf Pit Row ▲	1:64		$5
❑ Racing Champions	1:64		$15

	Scale	LE	Value
❑			
❑			
❑			
❑			

Note: *Jarrett's first Winston Cup start came in 1984.*

How Many: Total Value:

Page Totals:	How Many	Total Value

4

Interstate

	Scale	LE	Value
❑ Action	1:64		N/E
❑ Ertl	1:18		$72
❑ Funstuf Pit Row	1:43		$15
❑ Funstuf Pit Row	1:64		$10
❑ Matchbox/White Rose Super Stars ▲	1:64		$8
❑ Racing Champions	1:43		$18
❑ Racing Champions	1:64		$16
❑			
❑			
❑			

Note: *Dale Jarrett has an 8 handicap in golf.*

How Many: Total Value:

1993 Releases

5

PHOTO UNAVAILABLE

Interstate

	Scale	LE	Value
❑ Action/RCCA	1:64		$15
❑ Racing Champions	1:64		$20
❑ Racing Champions Premier	1:64		$27
❑ Racing Champions PVC Box (Daytona 500 Win)	1:64		$18
❑ Revell	1:24		$29
❑			

Note: *Dale Jarrett wore a Dallas Cowboys helmet when he won the 1993 Daytona 500.*

How Many: Total Value:

6

PHOTO UNAVAILABLE

Pic 'N Pay

	Scale	LE	Value
❑ Matchbox/White Rose Super Stars	1:64		$7
❑			
❑			
❑			
❑			

Note: *Jarrett won his first race after beating out second-place finisher Davey Allison by only eight inches.*

How Many: Total Value:

Page Totals:	How Many	Total Value

1994 Releases

7

Interstate

	Scale	LE	Value
❑ Action	1:64		N/E
❑ Action/RCCA	1:24		$200
❑ Action/RCCA	1:64		$30
❑ Racing Champions ▲	1:64		$24
❑ Racing Champions (yellow box)	1:64		$15
❑ Racing Champions Premier	1:64		$20
❑ Racing Champions Premier (Brickyard 400)	1:64		$28
❑			

How Many: | Total Value:

8

PHOTO UNAVAILABLE

Pic 'N Pay

	Scale	LE	Value
❑ Matchbox/White Rose Super Stars	1:64		$10
❑			
❑			
❑			
❑			

Note: In 1994, Jarrett lost the Winston Cup Championship by only 14 points.

How Many: | Total Value:

1995 Releases

9

PHOTO UNAVAILABLE

Mac Tools

	Scale	LE	Value
❑ Ertl	1:18		$82
❑ Revell	1:24		$45
❑			
❑			
❑			
❑			

How Many: | Total Value:

10

Texaco/Havoline

	Scale	LE	Value
❑ Action	1:24		$45
❑ Action	1:64		$18
❑ Action/RCCA	1:24		$55
❑ Action/RCCA	1:64		$28
❑ Ertl	1:18		$75
❑ Matchbox/White Rose Super Stars	1:64		$8
❑ Racing Champions ▲	1:24		$67
❑ Racing Champions	1:64		$14
❑ Racing Champions Premier	1:64		$17
❑ Racing Champions Promo	1:24		$70
❑ Racing Champions Promo	1:64		$20
❑ Racing Champions To The MAXX	1:64		$19
❑			

How Many: | Total Value:

Page Totals:	How Many	Total Value

1996 Releases

11

Band Aid

	Scale	LE	Value
❑ Racing Champions Promo ▲	1:64		$12
❑			

	Scale	LE	Value
❑			
❑			
❑			
❑			

Note: Dale Jarrett is one of four drivers who have won both the Busch Clash and the Daytona 500. He won these races in 1996.

How Many: **Total Value:**

12

Quality Care

	Scale	LE	Value
❑ Action ▲	1:24		$95
❑ Action	1:64		$17
❑ Action/RCCA	1:64		$30
❑ Matchbox/White Rose Super Stars	1:64		$9
❑ Racing Champions	1:18		$55
❑ Racing Champions	1:24		$48
❑ Racing Champions (hood open)	1:24		$53
❑ Racing Champions	1:64		$18
❑ Racing Champions (with emblem)	1:64		$20
❑ Racing Champions	1:144		$20
❑ Revell	1:24		$32
❑ Revell	1:64		$16
❑ Revell Collection	1:24		$58

	Scale	LE	Value
❑ Revell Collection	1:64		$20
❑			
❑			
❑			
❑			

Note: Dale Jarrett won the Brickyard 400 in 1996 and 1999.

How Many: **Total Value:**

13

Quality Care

	Scale	LE	Value
❑ Racing Champions Chrome Chase ▲	1:64		$140

	Scale	LE	Value
❑			
❑			
❑			
❑			

Note: Jarrett won the Daytona 500 in 1993 and 1996, narrowly beating out Dale Earnhardt both times.

How Many: **Total Value:**

Page Totals:	How Many	Total Value

1997 Releases

14

Gillette

	Scale	LE	Value
❑ Racing Champions	1:24		$26
❑ Racing Champions	1:64		N/E
❑ Racing Champions	1:144		N/E
❑ Racing Champions Roaring Racers	1:64		N/E
❑			
❑			
❑			

Note: *Dale Jarrett was named True Value Man Of The Year in 1997.*

How Many: Total Value:

15

Quality Care

	Scale	LE	Value
❑ Action	1:24		$70
❑ Action (Brickyard 400)	1:24		$85
❑ Action (Mac Tools)	1:24		$75
❑ Action	1:64		$16
❑ Action (Brickyard 400)	1:64		$16
❑ Action/RCCA	1:64		$24
❑ Action/RCCA Elite ▲	1:24		$200
❑ Ertl	1:18		$82
❑ Revell Club	1:18		$125
❑ Revell Collection	1:18		$95
❑ Revell Collection	1:43		$36
❑ Winner's Circle	1:24		$32
❑ Winner's Circle	1:64		$13
❑			

How Many: Total Value:

16

Quality Care (1996 paint scheme)

	Scale	LE	Value
❑ Winner's Circle	1:64		$14
❑			
❑			
❑			
❑			
❑			

Note: *Future Winston Cup champion Dale Jarrett didn't consider racing as a career until he was 20.*

How Many: Total Value:

17

White Rain

	Scale	LE	Value
❑ Action	1:64		$15
❑ Action/RCCA	1:24		$50
❑ Action/RCCA	1:64		$25
❑ Action/RCCA Elite	1:24		$145
❑ Racing Champions	1:24		$28
❑ Racing Champions ▲	1:64		$9
❑ Racing Champions	1:144		$6
❑ Revell Collection	1:24		$60
❑ Revell Hobby	1:64		$12
❑			

Note: *Jarrett names driving for the Wood Brothers in 1990 as his biggest career break.*

How Many: Total Value:

Page Totals:	How Many	Total Value

1998 Releases

18

Batman

	Scale	LE	Value
❑ Action	1:18		$100
❑ Action	1:24		$87
❑ Action	1:32		$60
❑ Action	1:64		$25
❑ Action/RCCA	1:64		$32
❑ Action/RCCA Elite ▲	1:24		$165
❑ Revell Club	1:18		$190
❑ Revell Club	1:24		$120
❑ Revell Collection	1:18		$95
❑ Revell Collection	1:24		$50
❑ Revell Collection	1:43		$48
❑ Revell Collection	1:64		$19
❑ Revell Select	1:18		$100
❑ Revell Select	1:24		$60
❑ Revell Select	1:43		$39
❑ Winner's Circle	1:43		$15
❑ Winner's Circle	1:64		$11
❑			
❑			
❑			
❑			

Note: *Dale Jarrett and his father, Ned, are the second father-son duo to win Winston Cup Championships.*

How Many:	Total Value:

19

Quality Care

	Scale	LE	Value
❑ Action	1:24		$78
❑ Action	1:32		$57
❑ Action	1:64		$16
❑ Action/RCCA	1:64		$28
❑ Action/RCCA (Fan Club)	1:64		$28
❑ Action/RCCA Elite ▲	1:24		$160
❑ Action/RCCA Elite (No Bull)	1:24		$155
❑ Revell Club	1:18		$165
❑ Revell Club	1:24		$135
❑ Revell Collection	1:18		$90
❑ Revell Collection	1:24		$75
❑ Revell Collection	1:43		$68
❑ Revell Collection	1:64		$20
❑ Revell Hobby	1:24		$50
❑ Winner's Circle	1:43		$15
❑ Winner's Circle	1:64		$10
❑			
❑			
❑			
❑			

How Many:	Total Value:

Page Totals:	How Many	Total Value

20

Quality Care

	Scale	LE	Value
❑ Action/RCCA Gold	1:32		$72
❑			
❑			
❑			
❑			
❑			

Note: Jarrett's previous jobs include working for the family lumber business, selling cars and operating a printing press.

How Many: | Total Value:

21

White Rain

	Scale	LE	Value
❑ Action ▲	1:24		$60
❑ Action	1:64		$16
❑ Action Promo	1:64		$15
❑ Action/RCCA	1:64		$24
❑ Action/RCCA Elite	1:24		$150
❑ Winner's Circle	1:64		$10
❑			
❑			
❑			
❑			

Note: Dale Jarrett was the first driver for the Joe Gibbs racing team.

How Many: | Total Value:

1999 Releases

22

Green Bay Packers

	Scale	LE	Value
❑ Action ▲	1:24		$100
❑ Action	1:64		$20
❑ Action/RCCA	1:64		$29
❑ Action/RCCA Elite	1:24		$200
❑ Revell Club	1:24		$96
❑ Revell Collection	1:24		$85
❑ Revell Collection	1:64		$24
❑			

Note: Jarrett's favorite sport after racing is football. He was the star quarterback for his high school team.

How Many: | Total Value:

Page Totals:	How Many	Total Value

23

Quality Care

	Scale	LE	Value
❑ Action	1:18		$120
❑ Action	1:24		$90
❑ Action (Last Lap)	1:24		$88
❑ Action	1:64		$15
❑ Action (Last Lap)	1:64		$22
❑ Action/RCCA	1:64		$23
❑ Action/RCCA (Last Lap)	1:64		$35
❑ Action/RCCA Elite	1:24		$180
❑ Action/RCCA Elite (Last Lap) ▲	1:24		$230
❑ Revell Club	1:24		$92
❑ Revell Collection	1:24		$75
❑ Revell Collection	1:64		$15
❑ Winner's Circle (No Bull)	1:64		$10
❑ Winner's Circle Speedweeks	1:64		$10
❑ Winner's Circle Tech Series	1:64		$10
❑			
❑			
❑			
❑			

Note: Jarrett lettered in four sports at Newton-Conover High School in North Carolina.

How Many: Total Value:

24

Quality Care

	Scale	LE	Value
❑ Action	1:24		$115
❑ Action	1:64		$20
❑ Action/RCCA	1:64		$30
❑ Action/RCCA Elite	1:24		$220
❑ Revell Club	1:24		$105
❑ Revell Collection ▲	1:24		$83
❑ Winner's Circle	1:64		$10
❑			
❑			
❑			
❑			

How Many: Total Value:

25

Quality Care 1999 Champ

	Scale	LE	Value
❑ Action ▲	1:24		$100
❑			
❑			
❑			
❑			
❑			

Note: Dale Jarrett was the 1999 NASCAR Winston Cup Champion.

How Many: Total Value:

Page Totals:	How Many	Total Value

26

Rayovac

	Scale	LE	Value
❑ Action ▲	1:24		$78
❑ Action	1:64		$18
❑ Revell Collection	1:24		$72
❑			
❑			
❑			
❑			

How Many: **Total Value:**

2000 Releases

27

Air Force

	Scale	LE	Value
❑ Action	1:10		N/E
❑ Action ▲	1:24		N/E
❑ Action	1:64		$16
❑ Action/RCCA Elite	1:24		$100
❑ Revell Club	1:24		$60
❑ Revell Collection	1:24		$75
❑ Revell Collection	1:64		$16
❑			
❑			

How Many: **Total Value:**

28

Quality Care

	Scale	LE	Value
❑ Action ▲	1:24		$60
❑ Action	1:64		$15
❑ Action/RCCA	1:64		$22
❑ Action/RCCA Elite	1:24		$140
❑ Revell Club	1:24		$60
❑ Winner's Circle Race Hood	1:64		$8
❑ Winner's Circle Sneak Preview	1:64		N/E
❑			

***Note:** Since 1996, Dale Jarrett has been the only Winston Cup driver to finish each year in the top three in points.*

How Many: **Total Value:**

Future Releases

Check our web site, ***CollectorsQuest.com***, for new Dale Jarrett product releases and record the information here.

Dale Jarrett®	Value	How Many	Total Value

Page Totals:	How Many	Total Value

Bobby Labonte™

Interstate Batteries has been Bobby Labonte's chief Winston Cup sponsor since 1995, but Interstate is not the only paint scheme Labonte fans can collect. Labonte has had several promotional paint schemes, including those promoting the movie *Small Soldiers*, Shell, MBNA and, most recently, the new children's cartoon *NASCAR Racers*. Fans of Labonte's Busch Series days will want to find die-cast replicas of his Dentyne and Maxwell House schemes. Die-cast models of Labonte's Hall Of Fame paint schemes from the mid-1990s are also highly prized among collectors.

1991 Releases

1

PHOTO UNAVAILABLE

Penrose

	Scale	LE	Value
❑ Action/RCCA	1:64		$32

	Scale	LE	Value
❑			
❑			
❑			
❑			

***Note:* In 1991, Labonte won the NASCAR Busch Series Grand National Division Championship.**

How Many: Total Value:

1992 Releases

2

PHOTO UNAVAILABLE

Penrose

	Scale	LE	Value
❑ Matchbox/White Rose Super Stars	1:64		$10

	Scale	LE	Value
❑			
❑			
❑			
❑			

***Note:* Labonte missed being the 1992 BGN champion by only three points.**

How Many: Total Value:

3

PHOTO UNAVAILABLE

Slim Jim

	Scale	LE	Value
❑ Matchbox/White Rose Super Stars	1:64		$10

	Scale	LE	Value
❑			
❑			
❑			
❑			

***Note:* Bobby Labonte raced quarter midgets when he was just 5 years old.**

How Many: Total Value:

Page Totals:	How Many	Total Value

1993 Releases

4

Maxwell House

	Scale	LE	Value
❑ Matchbox/White Rose Super Stars	1:64		$9

	Scale	LE	Value
❑ Racing Champions	1:24		$105
❑ Racing Champions	1:64		$34
❑			
❑			
❑			
❑			

Note: *Bobby Labonte won his first pole at Richmond in 1993.*

How Many: | Total Value:

1994 Releases

5

Dentyne

	Scale	LE	Value
❑ Racing Champions	1:24		$138
❑ Racing Champions	1:64		$120

	Scale	LE	Value
❑ Racing Champions Premier	1:64		$155
❑			
❑			
❑			
❑			

How Many: | Total Value:

6

Interstate

	Scale	LE	Value
❑ Racing Champions ▲	1:64		$15
❑			

	Scale	LE	Value
❑			
❑			
❑			
❑			

Note: *Labonte finished behind Jeff Gordon for the 1993 Rookie Of The Year.*

How Many: | Total Value:

7

Maxwell House

	Scale	LE	Value
❑ Racing Champions ▲	1:64		$36
❑ Racing Champions Premier	1:43		$37

	Scale	LE	Value
❑			
❑			
❑			
❑			

Note: *Bobby Labonte owns a Busch Grand National team, for which he acts as a team owner rather than a driver.*

How Many: | Total Value:

Page Totals:	How Many	Total Value

1995 Releases

8

Interstate

	Scale	LE	Value
❑ Matchbox/White Rose Super Stars	1:64		$11
❑ Racing Champions	1:18		$58
❑ Racing Champions	1:24		$50
❑ Racing Champions ▲	1:64		$19
❑ Racing Champions Matched Serial Numbers	1:64		$22
❑ Racing Champions Premier	1:64		$22
❑ Racing Champions To The MAXX	1:64		$27
❑ Revell	1:24		$38

How Many: Total Value:

1996 Releases

9

Interstate

	Scale	LE	Value
❑ Action	1:24		$95
❑ Action	1:64		$15
❑ Action/RCCA	1:64		$22
❑ Ertl (Easy Care)	1:18		$55
❑ Racing Champions ▲	1:24		$40
❑ Racing Champions	1:64		$15
❑ Racing Champions	1:144		$19
❑ Racing Champions Premier	1:18		N/E
❑ Racing Champions Premier with emblem	1:64		$20
❑ Racing Champions Preview	1:24		$30
❑ Racing Champions Preview	1:64		$15
❑ Revell	1:24		$35
❑ Revell	1:64		$13
❑ Revell Collection	1:24		$58
❑ Revell Collection	1:64		$20
❑			
❑			
❑			
❑			

***Note:** Bobby and Terry Labonte were the first brothers to occupy the front row in the Daytona 500.*

How Many: Total Value:

Page Totals:	How Many	Total Value

10

PHOTO UNAVAILABLE

Interstate

	Scale	LE	Value
❑ Racing Champions Chrome Chase	1:64		$120

	Scale	LE	Value
❑			
❑			
❑			
❑			

***Note:** Bobby Labonte's first Winston Cup win came in the 1995 Coca-Cola 600.*

How Many: | Total Value:

11

Joe Gibbs Pro Football Hall Of Fame

	Scale	LE	Value
❑ Action ▲	1:24		$130
❑ Action	1:64		$23

	Scale	LE	Value
❑ Action/RCCA	1:24		N/E
❑ Action/RCCA	1:64		$32
❑			
❑			
❑			
❑			

***Note:** Bobby Labonte first joined the Joe Gibbs Racing Team as Dale Jarrett's replacement.*

How Many: | Total Value:

12

Shell

	Scale	LE	Value
❑ Racing Champions	1:24		$55
❑ Racing Champions ▲	1:64		$15

	Scale	LE	Value
❑ Racing Champions Premier with emblem	1:64		$25
❑ Racing Champions Promo	1:64		$14
❑			
❑			
❑			
❑			

***Note:** Labonte's crew chief is Jimmy Makar.*

How Many: | Total Value:

Page Totals:	How Many	Total Value

1997 Releases

13

Interstate

	Scale	LE	Value
❑ Action	1:24		$72
❑ Action (Mac Tools) ▲	1:24		N/E
❑ Action	1:64		$17
❑ Action/RCCA	1:24		$50
❑ Action/RCCA	1:64		$22
❑ Action/RCCA Elite	1:24		$190
❑ Racing Champions	1:18		N/E
❑ Racing Champions	1:24		$32
❑ Racing Champions (hood open)	1:24		$30
❑ Racing Champions	1:64		$19
❑ Racing Champions	1:144		$7
❑ Racing Champions Pinnacle	1:64		$21
❑ Racing Champions Premier with emblem	1:64		$19
❑ Racing Champions Premier Preview with emblem	1:64		$18
❑ Racing Champions Preview	1:24		$40
❑ Racing Champions Preview	1:64		$20
❑ Racing Champions Preview	1:144		$9
❑ Racing Champions Roaring Racers	1:64		$20
❑ Revell	1:64		$11
❑ Revell (Texas)	1:64		$13
❑ Revell Club (Texas)	1:64		$100
❑ Revell Collection	1:18		$95
❑ Revell Collection (Texas)	1:18		$100
❑ Revell Collection	1:24		$58
❑ Revell Collection (Texas)	1:24		$95
❑ Revell Hobby	1:24		$72
❑ Revell Hobby (Texas)	1:24		$70
❑ Revell Hobby	1:64		$18
❑ Revell Hobby (Texas)	1:64		$17
❑ Winner's Circle	1:24		$32
❑ Winner's Circle	1:64		$12
❑			
❑			

Note: In 1997, Bobby Labonte won the NAPA 500 at the Atlanta Motor Speedway.

How Many: | Total Value:

14

Interstate

	Scale	LE	Value
❑ Racing Champions Chrome Chase with emblem ▲	1:64		$128
❑			
❑			
❑			
❑			

Note: Bobby Labonte holds the race record for the Coca-Cola 600 at Charlotte Motor Speedway, with a speed of 151.952 mph.

How Many: | Total Value:

15

Interstate

	Scale	LE	Value
❑ Racing Champions Premier Gold	1:18		$135
❑ Racing Champions Premier Gold Chrome	1:18		$275
❑ Racing Champions Premier Gold Chrome ▲	1:24		$300
❑ Racing Champions Premier Gold Chrome	1:64		$115
❑			
❑			
❑			

Note: In 1990, Labonte was the BGN Most Popular Driver and had four poles and five wins.

How Many: | Total Value:

Page Totals:	How Many	Total Value

1998 Releases

16

Hot Rod

	Scale	LE	Value
❑ Action ▲	1:24		$78
❑ Action	1:64		$25
❑ Action/RCCA	1:64		$30
❑ Action/RCCA Elite	1:24		$170
❑ Revell Club	1:18		$185
❑ Revell Club	1:24		$140
❑ Revell Collection	1:18		$94
❑ Revell Collection	1:24		$75
❑ Revell Collection	1:43		$35
❑ Revell Collection	1:64		$20
❑ Revell Select	1:24		$45
❑ Revell Select	1:64		$13
❑ Winner's Circle	1:64		$11
❑			
❑			
❑			
❑			
❑			
❑			
❑			

Note: Bobby Labonte's 1998 DieHard 500 win at the Talladega Speedway was the first win for a Pontiac since Richard Petty won the Winston 500 in 1983.

How Many: | Total Value:

17

Interstate

	Scale	LE	Value
❑ Action ▲	1:24		$78
❑ Action	1:64		$18
❑ Action/RCCA	1:64		$23
❑ Action/RCCA Elite	1:24		$145
❑ Revell Club	1:24		$92
❑ Revell Collection	1:24		$66
❑ Revell Collection	1:43		$32
❑ Revell Collection	1:64		$20
❑ Revell Select	1:24		$40
❑ Revell Select	1:64		$22
❑ Winner's Circle	1:24		$30
❑ Winner's Circle	1:64		$10
❑			

How Many: | Total Value:

18

PHOTO UNAVAILABLE

Interstate

	Scale	LE	Value
❑ Action/RCCA Gold	1:32		$68
❑			
❑			
❑			
❑			
❑			

Note: Labonte's first Winston Cup start was in 1991 at Dover.

How Many: | Total Value:

Page Totals:	How Many	Total Value

19

NASCAR Racers

	Scale	LE	Value
❑ Action	1:18		$102
❑			
❑			
❑			
❑			
❑			

Note: Labonte has won at least one race each year since 1995.

How Many: | Total Value:

20

Small Soldiers

	Scale	LE	Value
❑ Action ▲	1:24		$72
❑ Action	1:64		$24
❑ Action/RCCA	1:64		$30
❑ Action/RCCA Elite	1:24		$160
❑ Revell Club	1:18		$165
❑ Revell Club	1:24		$105
❑ Revell Collection	1:18		$90
❑ Revell Collection	1:24		$67
❑ Revell Collection	1:43		$34
❑ Revell Collection	1:64		$21
❑ Revell Select	1:64		$20
❑ Winner's Circle	1:24		$34
❑ Winner's Circle	1:64		$10
❑			

Note: In order to "protect his car," Labonte keeps toy soldiers in his car windows during races.

How Many: | Total Value:

1999 Releases

21

Interstate

	Scale	LE	Value
❑ Action ▲	1:24		$85
❑ Action	1:64		$15
❑ Action (Fan Club)	1:64		$12
❑ Action/RCCA	1:64		$24
❑ Action/RCCA Elite	1:24		$190
❑ Revell Club	1:24		$140
❑ Revell Collection	1:24		$75
❑ Revell Collection	1:64		$18
❑ Winner's Circle	1:64		$12
❑ Winner's Circle Speedweeks	1:43		$16
❑ Winner's Circle Speedweeks	1:64		$11

How Many: | Total Value:

22

MBNA

	Scale	LE	Value
❑ Action ▲	1:24		$72
❑ Action	1:64		$15
❑ Action/RCCA	1:64		$25
❑ Action/RCCA Elite	1:24		$160
❑			
❑			
❑			
❑			

Note: Labonte's best season came in 1999 when he scored five wins.

How Many: | Total Value:

Page Totals:	How Many	Total Value

23

NASCAR Racers

	Scale	LE	Value
❑ Action	1:18		$102
❑ Action	1:24		$75
❑ Action	1:64		$19
❑ Action/RCCA	1:64		$28
❑ Action/RCCA Elite ▲	1:24		$170
❑			
❑			
❑			
❑			

Note: Labonte says that racing nose-to-nose against his brother is harder than against a teammate.

How Many: Total Value:

2000 Releases

24

Interstate

	Scale	LE	Value
❑ Action	1:24		$82
❑ Action ▲	1:64		$18
❑ Action/RCCA	1:64		$27
❑ Action/RCCA Elite	1:24		$150
❑ Revell Club	1:24		$105
❑ Revell Collection	1:24		$80
❑ Revell Collection	1:64		$15
❑ Winner's Circle	1:64		$9
❑ Winner's Circle Deluxe	1:64		$12
❑ Winner's Circle Sneak Preview	1:24		$30
❑ Winner's Circle Sneak Preview	1:64		$11

How Many: Total Value:

25

MLB All-Star Game

	Scale	LE	Value
❑ Action/RCCA	1:64		$25
❑ Action/RCCA Elite ▲	1:24		$155
❑ Revell Club	1:24		$115
❑			
❑			
❑			
❑			

Note: Bobby Labonte often attends Carolina Panthers football games.

How Many: Total Value:

26

NASCAR Racers

	Scale	LE	Value
❑ Winner's Circle ▲	1:64		N/E
❑			
❑			
❑			
❑			
❑			

How Many: Total Value:

Page Totals:	How Many	Total Value

Future Releases

Check our web site, ***CollectorsQuest.com***, for new Bobby Labonte product releases and record the information here.

Bobby Labonte™	Value	How Many	Total Value

Page Totals:	How Many	Total Value

Future Releases

Check our web site, ***CollectorsQuest.com***, for new Bobby Labonte product releases and record the information here.

Bobby Labonte™	Value	How Many	Total Value

Page Totals:	How Many	Total Value

Mark Martin®

2000 saw a major change for Mark Martin's paint schemes. Since he did not renew his long-running contract with chief sponsor Valvoline, this will be the last year he drives the Valvoline car. Die-cast models of the last Valvoline paint jobs are likely to be highly sought after by collectors, as are the Winn-Dixie cars Martin drives on the Busch circuit. Although Martin does not run as many special paint schemes as other drivers, his charm and gentlemanly demeanor while racing ensure that his die-cast models will remain popular with fans.

1991 Releases

1

PHOTO UNAVAILABLE

Valvoline

	Scale	LE	Value
❑ Action/RCCA	1:64		N/E
❑			

	Scale	LE	Value
❑			
❑			
❑			
❑			

Note: Mark Martin's first career Winston Cup start came in 1981.

How Many: | Total Value:

1992 Releases

2

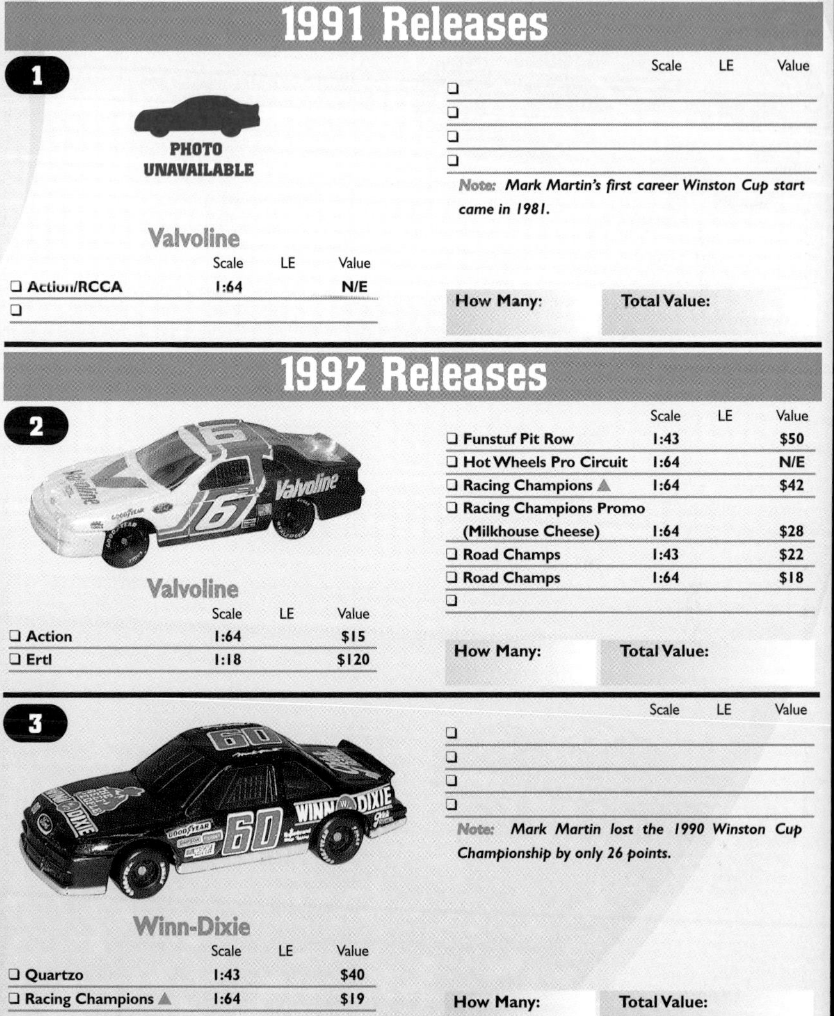

Valvoline

	Scale	LE	Value
❑ Action	1:64		$15
❑ Ertl	1:18		$120

	Scale	LE	Value
❑ Funstuf Pit Row	1:43		$50
❑ Hot Wheels Pro Circuit	1:64		N/E
❑ Racing Champions ▲	1:64		$42
❑ Racing Champions Promo (Milkhouse Cheese)	1:64		$28
❑ Road Champs	1:43		$22
❑ Road Champs	1:64		$18
❑			

How Many: | Total Value:

3

Winn-Dixie

	Scale	LE	Value
❑ Quartzo	1:43		$40
❑ Racing Champions ▲	1:64		$19

	Scale	LE	Value
❑			
❑			
❑			
❑			

Note: Mark Martin lost the 1990 Winston Cup Championship by only 26 points.

How Many: | Total Value:

Page Totals:	How Many	Total Value

1993 Releases

4

Folgers

	Scale	LE	Value
❑ Action/RCCA Promo ▲	1:64		$50
❑			
❑			
❑			
❑			

How Many: Total Value:

5

Valvoline

	Scale	LE	Value
❑ Action	1:64		$15
❑ Matchbox/White Rose Super Stars	1:64		$12
❑ Racing Champions	1:24		$80
❑ Racing Champions	1:43		$45
❑ Racing Champions	1:64		$24
❑ Racing Champions Premier	1:43		$55
❑ Racing Champions Premier ▲	1:64		$47
❑ Racing Champions Premier (4 In A Row Promo)	1:64		$45
❑ Racing Champions PVC Box Premier (8/15/93)	1:64		N/E
❑ Racing Champions PVC Box Premier (Bristol 8/28/93)	1:64		N/E
❑ Racing Champions PVC Box Premier (Darlington 9/5/93)	1:64		N/E
❑ Racing Champions PVC Box Premier (Watkins Glen 8/8/93)	1:64		N/E
❑ Revell	1:24		$34
❑			
❑			
❑			
❑			

Note: Mark Martin won four consecutive Winston Cup races in 1993.

How Many: Total Value:

6

Winn Dixie

	Scale	LE	Value
❑ Racing Champions ▲	1:43		$25
❑ Racing Champions	1:64		$14
❑ Racing Champions Premier	1:43		$40
❑ Racing Champions Premier	1:64		$32
❑ Revell	1:24		$60
❑			
❑			
❑			
❑			

Note: In 1982, Martin came in second place for the Rookie Of The Year award, behind Geoff Bodine.

How Many: Total Value:

Page Totals:	How Many	Total Value

1994 Releases

7

Valvoline

	Scale	LE	Value
❑ Action	1:64		$23
❑ Matchbox/White Rose Super Stars	1:64		$10
❑ Raceway Replicas	1:24		$190
❑ Racing Champions	1:24		$65
❑ Racing Champions	1:64		$26
❑ Racing Champions (100 Years Of Racing)	1:64		$35
❑ Racing Champions Hobby	1:64		$28
❑ Racing Champions Premier	1:43		$36
❑ Racing Champions Premier	1:64		$48
❑ Racing Champions Premier (4 In A Row Promo)	1:64		$56
❑ Racing Champions Premier (Brickyard 400)	1:64		$75
❑ Racing Champions To The MAXX	1:64		$30
❑			
❑			
❑			
❑			

Note: *During a BGN race in Bristol in 1994, Martin drove into Victory Lane one lap early because he confused the white and yellow flag for a checkered one.*

How Many:	Total Value:

8

Winn Dixie

	Scale	LE	Value
❑ Ertl (by GMP)	1:18		$92
❑ Matchbox/White Rose Super Stars ▲	1:64		$12
❑ Racing Champions	1:43		$23
❑ Racing Champions	1:64		$20
❑ Racing Champions Premier	1:43		$38
❑ Racing Champions Premier	1:64		$30
❑ Revell Collection	1:24		$48
❑			
❑			
❑			

Note: *Mark Martin's first win came after six second-place finishes.*

How Many:	Total Value:

1995 Releases

9

Folgers

	Scale	LE	Value
❑ Action ▲	1:24		N/E
❑ Action	1:64		$65
❑ Action/RCCA	1:24		$430
❑			
❑			
❑			
❑			

How Many:	Total Value:

Page Totals:	How Many	Total Value

10

Valvoline

	Scale	LE	Value
❑ Action	1:24		$100
❑ Action (Brickyard)	1:24		$120
❑ Action	1:64		$24
❑ Action (100 Years Of Racing)	1:64		$30
❑ Action (Brickyard 400)	1:64		$22
❑ Action/RCCA	1:24		N/E
❑ Action/RCCA	1:64		$35
❑ Action/RCCA (Brickyard 400)	1:64		$30
❑ Matchbox/White Rose Super Stars	1:64		$8
❑ Racing Champions	1:24		$50
❑ Racing Champions ▲	1:64		$24
❑ Racing Champions Matched Serial Numbers	1:64		$28
❑ Racing Champions Premier	1:64		$42
❑ Racing Champions Preview	1:24		$58
❑ Racing Champions Preview	1:64		$30
❑ Racing Champions To The MAXX	1:64		$32
❑ Revell	1:24		$36
❑			
❑			
❑			
❑			

How Many: | Total Value:

11

Winn Dixie

	Scale	LE	Value
❑ Racing Champions Premier	1:43		$28
❑ Racing Champions Premier ▲	1:64		$22
❑			
❑			
❑			
❑			

How Many: | Total Value:

1996 Releases

12

PHOTO UNAVAILABLE

Durablend

	Scale	LE	Value
❑ Racing Champions	1:24		$45
❑ Racing Champions	1:64		$24
❑ Revell Collection	1:64		$20
❑			
❑			
❑			
❑			

How Many: | Total Value:

Page Totals:	How Many	Total Value

13

Miller

	Scale	LE	Value
❑ Action	1:24		$125
❑ Action ▲	1:64		$27
❑ Action/RCCA	1:64		N/E
❑			
❑			
❑			
❑			

How Many: | Total Value:

14

Valvoline

	Scale	LE	Value
❑ Action	1:24		$125
❑ Action	1:64		$18
❑ Action/RCCA	1:64		$32
❑ Ertl	1:18		$78
❑ Matchbox/White Rose Super Stars	1:64		$12
❑ Racing Champions	1:24		$42
❑ Racing Champions (hood open)	1:24		$60
❑ Racing Champions	1:64		$20
❑ Racing Champions	1:144		$25
❑ Racing Champions Premier	1:64		N/E
❑ Racing Champions Preview ▲	1:24		$48
❑ Racing Champions Preview	1:64		$26
❑ Racing Champions Promo (Roush Racing box)	1:24		$35
❑ Revell	1:24		$32
❑ Revell	1:64		$13
❑ Revell Collection	1:24		$55
❑ Revell Collection	1:64		$19
❑			
❑			
❑			
❑			

How Many: | Total Value:

15

Valvoline

	Scale	LE	Value
❑ Racing Champions Chrome Chase ▲	1:64		$170
❑			
❑			
❑			
❑			

Note: Mark Martin has won over $1 million each year since 1989.

How Many: | Total Value:

Page Totals:	How Many	Total Value

16

Winn Dixie

	Scale	LE	Value
❑ Racing Champions	1:64		$14
❑ Racing Champions Premier	1:18		$40
❑			
❑			
❑			
❑			

Note: *Martin co-wrote a book on fitness for drivers.*

How Many: Total Value:

1997 Releases

17

Valvoline

	Scale	LE	Value
❑ Action	1:24		$100
❑ Action (Mac Tools)	1:24		$130
❑ Action	1:64		$20
❑ Action/RCCA	1:64		$35
❑ Action/RCCA Elite	1:24		$225
❑ Ertl	1:18		$75
❑ Hot Wheels	1:64		$6
❑ Hot Wheels Collector	1:64		$8
❑ Hot Wheels Short Track	1:64		$8
❑ Hot Wheels Superspeedway	1:64		$8
❑ Racing Champions	1:24		$38
❑ Racing Champions (hood open)	1:24		$40
❑ Racing Champions	1:64		$17
❑ Racing Champions	1:144		$15
❑ Racing Champions Pinnacle	1:64		$24
❑ Racing Champions Premier with emblem	1:64		$22
❑ Racing Champions Previews ▲	1:24		$46
❑ Racing Champions Previews	1:64		$22
❑ Racing Champions Previews	1:144		$13
❑ Racing Champions Roaring Racers	1:64		$24
❑ Revell	1:24		$38
❑ Revell Club	1:18		N/E
❑ Revell Club	1:24		N/E
❑ Revell Collection	1:18		$85
❑ Revell Collection	1:24		$75
❑ Revell Collection	1:43		$43
❑ Revell Hobby	1:24		$35
❑ Revell Hobby	1:64		$17
❑			
❑			
❑			

How Many: Total Value:

Page Totals: How Many | Total Value

18

Valvoline

	Scale	LE	Value
❑ Racing Champions Premier Gold	1:18		$230
❑ Racing Champions Premier Gold	1:64		$35
❑ Racing Champions Premier Gold Chrome	1:18		$400
❑ Racing Champions Premier Gold Chrome ▲	1:64		$200
❑			
❑			

Note: In 1997, Martin placed third in the Winston Cup standings and finished a mere 29 points behind the winner.

How Many: | Total Value:

19

Winn Dixie

	Scale	LE	Value
❑ Action	1:64		$20
❑ Action/RCCA	1:24		$95
❑ Action/RCCA	1:64		$28
❑ Action/RCCA Elite ▲	1:24		$220
❑ Racing Champions	1:64		$8
❑ Racing Champions	1:144		N/E
❑ Revell Collection	1:18		$115
❑ Revell Collection	1:24		$90
❑ Revell Collection (Texas Win)	1:24		$100
❑			
❑			

How Many: | Total Value:

1998 Releases

20

Eagle One

	Scale	LE	Value
❑ Hot Wheels Collector	1:64		$9
❑ Hot Wheels Preview	1:64		$9
❑ Hot Wheels Promo	1:64		N/E
❑ Hot Wheels Track	1:64		$16
❑ Racing Champions	1:24		$44
❑ Racing Champions	1:64		$30
❑ Racing Champions Authentics ▲	1:24		$94
❑ Racing Champions Press Pass	1:64		$24
❑			

How Many: | Total Value:

21

PHOTO UNAVAILABLE

Eagle One

	Scale	LE	Value
❑ Racing Champions Chrome Chase	1:64		$145
❑ Racing Champions Chrome Signature	1:64		N/E
❑			
❑			
❑			
❑			

How Many: | Total Value:

COLLECTOR'S VALUE GUIDE™

Page Totals:	How Many	Total Value

22

Eagle One

	Scale	LE	Value
❑ Racing Champions 24K Gold	1:24		$105

	Scale	LE	Value
❑ Racing Champions 24K Gold	1:64		$50
❑ Racing Champions Gold	1:24		$86
❑ Racing Champions Gold with emblem	1:64		$40
❑ Racing Champions Toys 'R Us Gold ▲	1:64		$20
❑			
❑			
❑			

How Many: Total Value:

23

Eagle One

	Scale	LE	Value
❑ Racing Champions Platinum ▲	1:24		$70

	Scale	LE	Value
❑ Racing Champions Platinum	1:64		N/E
❑			
❑			
❑			
❑			

How Many: Total Value:

24

Hot Wheels

	Scale	LE	Value
❑ Hot Wheels ▲	1:24		$45
❑			

	Scale	LE	Value
❑			
❑			
❑			
❑			

How Many: Total Value:

25

PHOTO UNAVAILABLE

Kosei

	Scale	LE	Value
❑ Racing Champions	1:24		$115
❑ Racing Champions	1:64		$38

	Scale	LE	Value
❑			
❑			
❑			
❑			

Note: In 1998, Mark Martin became the first driver to win a Winston Cup race in a Ford Taurus. The victory came March 1 at the Las Vegas 400.

How Many: Total Value:

Page Totals:	How Many	Total Value

26

SynPower

	Scale	LE	Value
❑ Hot Wheels Collector	1:64		$25
❑ Hot Wheels Promo	1:64		$14
❑ Hot Wheels Track	1:64		$17
❑ Racing Champions	1:24		$68
❑ Racing Champions	1:64		$26
❑ Racing Champions Authentics ▲	1:24		$94
❑			
❑			
❑			
❑			

How Many: Total Value:

27

SynPower

	Scale	LE	Value
❑ Racing Champions Gold ▲	1:24		$105
❑ Racing Champions Gold (hood open)	1:24		$100
❑ Racing Champions Gold with emblem	1:64		$39
❑			
❑			
❑			
❑			

Note: Mark Martin has won more BGN victories than anyone else in history.

How Many: Total Value:

28

SynPower

	Scale	LE	Value
❑ Racing Champions Platinum	1:24		$60
❑ Racing Champions Platinum	1:64		$26
❑			
❑			
❑			
❑			

How Many: Total Value:

Page Totals:	How Many	Total Value

29

Valvoline

	Scale	LE	Value
❑ Hot Wheels	1:24		$33
❑ Hot Wheels	1:43		$18
❑ Hot Wheels Collector ▲	1:64		$7
❑ Hot Wheels Pit Crew	1:64		$10
❑ Hot Wheels Preview	1:64		$9
❑ Hot Wheels Track	1:64		$17
❑ Hot Wheels Trading Paint	1:64		$16
❑ Racing Champions	1:24		$37
❑ Racing Champions	1:64		$17
❑ Racing Champions	1:144		$11
❑ Racing Champions Authentics	1:24		$82
❑ Racing Champions Pinnacle	1:64		$20
❑ Racing Champions Signature	1:24		$33
❑ Racing Champions Signature	1:64		$19
❑			
❑			
❑			
❑			

How Many: Total Value:

30

Valvoline

	Scale	LE	Value
❑ Racing Champions Chrome Chase ▲	1:64		$135
❑			
❑			
❑			
❑			

Note: Martin has won four ASA championships.

How Many: Total Value:

31

Valvoline

	Scale	LE	Value
❑ Racing Champions 24K Gold	1:24		$102
❑ Racing Champions 24K Gold	1:64		$50
❑ Racing Champions Gold	1:24		$80
❑ Racing Champions Gold (hood open)	1:24		$100
❑ Racing Champions Gold with emblem	1:64		$36
❑ Racing Champions Reflections in Gold ▲	1:24		$92
❑ Racing Champions Reflections in Gold	1:64		$43
❑ Racing Champions Toys 'R Us Gold	1:64		$22

How Many: Total Value:

Page Totals:	How Many	Total Value

32

Valvoline

	Scale	LE	Value
❑ Racing Champions Platinum	1:24		$65
❑ Racing Champions Platinum	1:64		$14
❑			
❑			
❑			
❑			

How Many: Total Value:

33

Winn Dixie

	Scale	LE	Value
❑ Racing Champions	1:64		$14
❑ Racing Champions Press Pass	1:64		$15
❑ Racing Champions Promo	1:64		$13
❑			
❑			
❑			
❑			

Note: The same year Mark Martin won his first race (1989), he also received the National Motorsports Press Association Driver Of The Year award.

How Many: Total Value:

34

PHOTO
UNAVAILABLE

Winn Dixie

	Scale	LE	Value
❑ Racing Champions Chrome Chase	1:64		$82
❑			
❑			
❑			
❑			

How Many: Total Value:

35

Winn Dixie

	Scale	LE	Value
❑ Racing Champions Gold	1:24		$80
❑ Racing Champions Gold ▲	1:64		$37
❑ Racing Champions Reflections in Gold	1:24		$78
❑ Racing Champions Reflections in Gold	1:64		$37
❑ Racing Champions Toys 'R Us Gold	1:64		$15
❑			
❑			
❑			
❑			

How Many: Total Value:

Page Totals:	How Many	Total Value

36

Winn Dixie

	Scale	LE	Value
❑ Racing Champions Platinum	1:24		$25
❑ Racing Champions Platinum ▲	1:64		$10
❑			
❑			
❑			
❑			

How Many: Total Value:

1999 Releases

37

Eagle One

	Scale	LE	Value
❑ Racing Champions Authentics	1:24		$100
❑ Racing Champions NASCAR Rules!	1:64		$27
❑ Racing Champions Premier (Mac Tools) ▲	1:24		$30
❑ Racing Champions Signature	1:64		$15
❑ Team Caliber	1:24		$170
❑ Team Caliber Roush Signature Series	1:64		$33
❑			

How Many: Total Value:

38

PHOTO UNAVAILABLE

Hot Wheels

	Scale	LE	Value
❑ Hot Wheels	1:24		$45
❑			
❑			
❑			
❑			
❑			

How Many: Total Value:

39

J-Mar Express

	Scale	LE	Value
❑ Action/RCCA Elite ▲	1:24		$190
❑			
❑			
❑			
❑			
❑			

How Many: Total Value:

Page Totals:	How Many	Total Value

40

Jim Magill

	Scale	LE	Value
❑ Action	1:24		$50
❑ Action/RCCA Elite ▲	1:24		$100

	Scale	LE	Value
❑			
❑			
❑			
❑			

Note: *Martin did not miss a single race in 1999, despite suffering a broken wrist and kneecap and several fractured ribs.*

How Many: | Total Value:

41

PHOTO UNAVAILABLE

Jim Magill (orange)

	Scale	LE	Value
❑ Action	1:24		$45
❑ Action/RCCA Elite	1:24		$160

	Scale	LE	Value
❑			
❑			
❑			
❑			

How Many: | Total Value:

42

PHOTO UNAVAILABLE

SynPower

	Scale	LE	Value
❑ Racing Champions Authentics	1:24		N/E

	Scale	LE	Value
❑			
❑			
❑			
❑			

How Many: | Total Value:

Page Totals:	How Many	Total Value

43

Valvoline

	Scale	LE	Value
❑ Hot Wheels	1:24		$20
❑ Hot Wheels	1:43		$17
❑ Hot Wheels Collector	1:64		$7
❑ Hot Wheels Collector (Daytona 500 Edition)	1:64		$7
❑ Hot Wheels Crew's Choice	1:24		$48
❑ Hot Wheels Crew's Choice	1:43		$23
❑ Hot Wheels Deluxe Black Chrome	1:24		$47
❑ Hot Wheels Speed and Thunder	1:64		N/E
❑ Hot Wheels Track Edition	1:64		$20
❑ Hot Wheels Trading Paint	1:64		$26
❑ Racing Champions	1:24		$31
❑ Racing Champions	1:64		$15
❑ Racing Champions 3-D	1:64		$22
❑ Racing Champions Authentics	1:24		$88
❑ Racing Champions NASCAR Rules!	1:64		$25
❑ Racing Champions Premier (Mac Tools)	1:24		N/E
❑ Racing Champions Press Pass	1:64		$18
❑ Racing Champions Signature Driver Series	1:24		$39
❑ Racing Champions Signature Driver Series	1:64		$10
❑ Racing Champions Under The Lights	1:24		$48
❑ Racing Champions Under The Lights	1:64		$21
❑ Team Caliber Roush Signature ▲	1:24		$132
❑ Team Caliber Roush Signature	1:64		$35
❑			
❑			
❑			
❑			

How Many: Total Value:

44

Valvoline

	Scale	LE	Value
❑ Racing Champions Chrome Chase ▲	1:24		$90
❑ Racing Champions Chrome Chase	1:64		$60
❑ Racing Champions Chrome Signature	1:24		$80
❑ Racing Champions Chrome Signature	1:64		$42
❑ Racing Champions Toys 'R Us Chrome Chase	1:64		$25
❑			
❑			

How Many: Total Value:

45

Valvoline

	Scale	LE	Value
❑ Racing Champions 24K Gold	1:24		$79
❑ Racing Champions 24K Gold	1:64		$40
❑ Racing Champions Gold	1:24		$46
❑ Racing Champions Gold	1:64		$32
❑ Racing Champions Gold with emblem ▲	1:64		$35
❑			
❑			
❑			
❑			

How Many: Total Value:

Page Totals:	How Many	Total Value

46

PHOTO UNAVAILABLE

Valvoline

	Scale	LE	Value
❑ Racing Champions Platinum	1:24		$75
❑ Racing Champions Platinum	1:64		$38
❑ Racing Champions Precious Metals Team Colors	1:64		N/E
❑			
❑			
❑			
❑			

How Many: Total Value:

47

Winn Dixie

	Scale	LE	Value
❑ Race Image Dimension 4	1:32		N/E
❑ Racing Champions	1:24		$45
❑ Racing Champions	1:64		$16
❑ Racing Champions Authentics ▲	1:24		$92
❑ Racing Champions NASCAR Rules!	1:64		$23
❑ Racing Champions Signature Driver Series	1:64		$18
❑ Racing Champions Under The Lights	1:64		N/E
❑			

How Many: Total Value:

48

PHOTO UNAVAILABLE

Winn Dixie

	Scale	LE	Value
❑ Racing Champions Chrome Chase	1:64		$42
❑			
❑			
❑			
❑			

Note: In almost twenty years on the Winston Cup race circuit, Mark Martin has yet to win a Winston Cup Championship.

How Many: Total Value:

49

PHOTO UNAVAILABLE

Winn Dixie

	Scale	LE	Value
❑ Racing Champions 24K Gold	1:64		$22
❑ Racing Champions Gold	1:24		$45
❑ Racing Champions Gold with emblem	1:64		$38
❑			
❑			
❑			
❑			

How Many: Total Value:

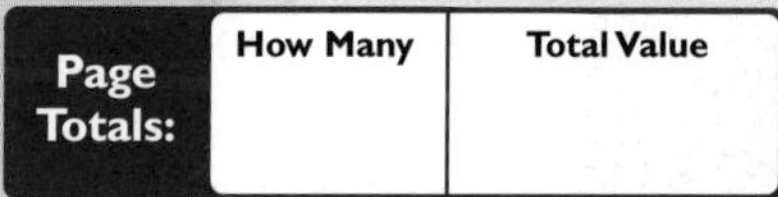

Page Totals:	How Many	Total Value

50

Zerex

	Scale	LE	Value
❑ Race Image Dimension 4	1:32		N/E
❑ Racing Champions	1:24		$36
❑ Racing Champions	1:64		$17
❑ Racing Champions 3-D	1:64		N/E
❑ Racing Champions Authentics ▲	1:24		$94
❑ Racing Champions NASCAR Rules!	1:64		$25
❑ Racing Champions Signature Driver Series	1:64		N/E
❑ Racing Champions Under The Lights	1:24		N/E
❑			

How Many: Total Value:

51

Zerex

	Scale	LE	Value
❑ Racing Champions Chrome Chase	1:24		$115
❑ Racing Champions Chrome Chase ▲	1:64		$46
❑ Racing Champions Chrome Signature Driver Series	1:64		$38
❑ Racing Champions Silver Chrome (QVC Exclusive)	1:24		N/E
❑ Racing Champions Silver Chrome (QVC Exclusive)	1:64		N/E
❑			

How Many: Total Value:

52

Zerex

	Scale	LE	Value
❑ Race Image Dimension 4 Gold ▲	1:32		N/E
❑ Racing Champions 24K Gold	1:24		N/E
❑ Racing Champions 24K Gold	1:64		N/E
❑			
❑			
❑			
❑			

How Many: Total Value:

Page Totals:	How Many	Total Value

2000 Releases

53

Eagle One

	Scale	LE	Value
❑ Race Image Dimension 4	1:32		N/E
❑ Racing Champions	1:64		$15

	Scale	LE	Value
❑ Team Caliber Owner's Series ▲	1:24		$140
❑ Team Caliber Owner's Series	1:64		$35
❑ Team Caliber Preferred	1:24		$88
❑			
❑			

How Many: **Total Value:**

54

Enduro/Activision

	Scale	LE	Value
❑ Action ▲	1:24		$75
❑ Action	1:64		$30

	Scale	LE	Value
❑ Action/RCCA	1:64		$20
❑ Action/RCCA Elite	1:24		$85
❑			
❑			
❑			
❑			

Note: Through 1999, Mark Martin has not ended a season below sixth place in the Winston Cup point standings since 1988.

How Many: **Total Value:**

55

Jim Magill

	Scale	LE	Value
❑ Action	1:24		$95
❑ Action ▲	1:64		$16

	Scale	LE	Value
❑ Action/RCCA	1:64		$20
❑ Action/RCCA Elite	1:24		$100
❑			
❑			
❑			
❑			

Note: The Jim Magill and Enduro/Activision cars were originally raced by Martin during the 1983 season.

How Many: **Total Value:**

56

Jim Magill

	Scale	LE	Value
❑ Action ▲	1:24		$95
❑ Action	1:64		$16

	Scale	LE	Value
❑ Action/RCCA	1:64		$20
❑ Action/RCCA Elite	1:24		$100
❑			
❑			
❑			
❑			

How Many: **Total Value:**

Page Totals:	How Many	Total Value

57

Max Life

	Scale	LE	Value
❑ Team Caliber Owner's Series ▲	1:24		$70
❑ Team Caliber Preferred	1:24		$60
❑			
❑			
❑			
❑			

Note: On the Winston Cup circuit, Martin has 31 wins in his last 13 full seasons.

How Many: Total Value:

58

Valvoline

	Scale	LE	Value
❑ Hot Wheels Deluxe	1:24		N/E
❑ Race Image Dimension 4	1:32		N/E
❑ Racing Champions	1:24		$25
❑ Racing Champions	1:64		$8
❑ Racing Champions NASCAR Rules!	1:64		$20
❑ Racing Champions Premier	1:24		$40
❑ Racing Champions Premier	1:64		$12
❑ Racing Champions War Paint	1:24		N/E
❑ Racing Champions War Paint	1:64		N/E
❑ Team Caliber Owner's Series ▲	1:24		$106
❑ Team Caliber Owner's Series	1:64		$20
❑ Team Caliber Preferred	1:24		$98
❑ Team Caliber White Knuckle	1:24		$32
❑ Team Caliber White Knuckle	1:64		$15
❑			
❑			
❑			
❑			

How Many: Total Value:

59

PHOTO UNAVAILABLE

Valvoline

	Scale	LE	Value
❑ Racing Champions Chrome Chase	1:24		$60
❑ Racing Champions Chrome Chase	1:64		$25
❑			
❑			
❑			
❑			

How Many: Total Value:

Page Totals:	How Many	Total Value

60

Valvoline

	Scale	LE	Value
❑ Racing Champions Time Trial ▲	1:24		$33

	Scale	LE	Value
❑ Racing Champions Time Trial	1:64		$16
❑			
❑			
❑			
❑			

How Many: Total Value:

61

Winn Dixie

	Scale	LE	Value
❑ Ertl Proshop	1:24		N/E
❑ Racing Champions ▲	1:64		$12

	Scale	LE	Value
❑ Team Caliber	1:24		$75
❑			
❑			
❑			
❑			

How Many: Total Value:

Future Releases

Check our web site, ***CollectorsQuest.com***, for new Mark Martin product releases and record the information here.

Mark Martin®	Value	How Many	Total Value

Page Totals:	How Many	Total Value

Tony Stewart®

Tony Stewart is a relative newcomer to the world of NASCAR, and though he does not yet have a great number of die-cast, the ones that do exist are sure to be collector favorites. Home Depot is Stewart's main sponsor, but one of his cars has also featured a paint scheme promoting the movie *Small Soldiers* (along with teammate Bobby Labonte). He has also, in collaboration with Home Depot, run special paint schemes to promote the charitable organization Habitat For Humanity.

1998 Releases

1

Shell

	Scale	LE	Value
❑ Action	1:24		$125
❑ Action	1:64		$38
❑ Action/RCCA	1:18		$60
❑ Action/RCCA	1:64		$48
❑ Action/RCCA Elite	1:24		$250
❑ Revell Club	1:18		$195
❑ Revell Club	1:24		$180
❑ Revell Collection ▲	1:18		$110
❑ Revell Collection	1:24		$100
❑ Revell Collection	1:64		$36
❑ Revell Select	1:24		N/E
❑ Revell Select	1:64		$30
❑ Winner's Circle	1:64		$17
❑			
❑			
❑			
❑			
❑			
❑			
❑			

Note: *In 1995, Tony Stewart became the first driver to win the Triple Crown from the United States Auto Club (USAC).*

How Many: | **Total Value:**

2

Small Soldiers

	Scale	LE	Value
❑ Action	1:24		$98
❑ Action	1:64		$30
❑ Action/RCCA	1:64		$42
❑ Action/RCCA Elite	1:24		$188
❑ Revell Club	1:18		$165
❑ Revell Club	1:24		$125
❑ Revell Collection	1:18		$90
❑ Revell Collection ▲	1:24		$84
❑ Revell Collection	1:43		$35
❑ Revell Collection	1:64		$34
❑ Revell Select	1:64		$25
❑ Winner's Circle	1:24		$39
❑ Winner's Circle	1:64		$16
❑			

How Many: | **Total Value:**

Page Totals:	How Many	Total Value

1999 Releases

3

Habitat For Humanity

	Scale	LE	Value
❑ Action	1:18		$140
❑ Action	1:24		$90
❑ Action	1:64		$28
❑ Action/RCCA	1:64		$40
❑ Action/RCCA Elite ▲	1:24		$275
❑ Action/RCCA Elite SelectNet	1:24		$170
❑ Revell Club	1:18		$170
❑ Revell Club	1:24		$165
❑ Revell Collection	1:18		$110
❑ Revell Collection	1:24		$110
❑ Revell Collection	1:43		$32
❑ Revell Collection	1:64		$35

How Many: Total Value:

4

Home Depot

	Scale	LE	Value
❑ Action	1:18		$185
❑ Action	1:24		$350
❑ Action (black window, employee car)	1:24		$225
❑ Action	1:32		$110
❑ Action	1:64		$65
❑ Action Promo (clear window box)	1:24		$125
❑ Action Promo (hood open)	1:24		$125
❑ Action/RCCA	1:32		$45
❑ Action/RCCA	1:64		$85
❑ Action/RCCA Elite	1:24		$640
❑ Action/RCCA Elite Selectnet ▲	1:24		$250
❑ Action/RCCA Selectnet	1:64		$35
❑ Revell Club	1:24		$300
❑ Revell Collection	1:18		$225
❑ Revell Collection	1:24		$220
❑ Revell Collection	1:64		$60
❑ Winner's Circle	1:24		$48
❑ Winner's Circle	1:43		$30
❑ Winner's Circle	1:64		$36
❑			
❑			
❑			
❑			

Note: In May of 1999, Stewart became the first driver to complete both the Indianapolis 500 and the Coca-Cola 600 on the same day.

How Many: Total Value:

5

Home Depot

	Scale	LE	Value
❑ Action 24K Gold (QVC Exclusive) ▲	1:24		$100
❑			
❑			
❑			
❑			

Note: As far as the number of races won and the number of points earned, Tony Stewart's rookie year was the greatest in the history of the Winston Cup series.

How Many: Total Value:

Page Totals:	How Many	Total Value

6

Home Depot – Fan Club

	Scale	LE	Value
❑ Action	1:24		$275
❑			
❑			
❑			
❑			
❑			

Note: *In 1999, Stewart's hometown of Columbus, Indiana awarded him the key to the city and celebrated "Tony Stewart Day."*

How Many: | Total Value:

2000 Releases

7

Habitat For Humanity

	Scale	LE	Value
❑ Winner's Circle Deluxe with emblem ▲	1:64		$11
❑			
❑			
❑			
❑			

Note: *Tony Stewart raced a car promoting Habitat For Humanity on October 11, 1999.*

How Many: | Total Value:

8

Home Depot

	Scale	LE	Value
❑ Action ▲	1:18		$110
❑ Action	1:24		$87
❑ Action (Brickyard 400)	1:24		N/E
❑ Action	1:64		$20
❑ Action/RCCA	1:64		$30
❑ Action/RCCA Elite	1:24		$185
❑ Action/RCCA Elite (Rookie Of The Year)	1:24		$180
❑ Revell Club	1:18		$120
❑ Revell Club (Rookie Of The Year)	1:18		$120
❑ Revell Club	1:24		$110
❑ Revell Club (Rookie Of The Year)	1:24		$115
❑ Revell Collection (Rookie Of The Year)	1:18		$95
❑ Revell Collection	1:24		$75
❑ Revell Collection (Rookie Of The Year)	1:24		$100
❑ Revell Collection (Rookie Of The Year)	1:43		$35
❑ Revell Collection	1:64		$28
❑ Revell Collection (Rookie Of The Year)	1:64		$26
❑ Winner's Circle	1:24		$33
❑ Winner's Circle	1:43		$18
❑ Winner's Circle (First Win)	1:64		$12
❑ Winner's Circle (Rookie Record Breaker)	1:64		$13
❑ Winner's Circle Deluxe with emblem	1:64		$12
❑ Winner's Circle New Stars	1:64		$12
❑ Winner's Circle Sneak Preview Series (First Win)	1:64		$14
❑			
❑			
❑			

Note: *Stewart won the outside pole for his first Daytona 500.*

How Many: | Total Value:

Page Totals:	How Many	Total Value

9

Home Depot

	Scale	LE	Value
❑ Action 24K Gold (Rookie Of The Year, QVC Exclusive) ▲	1:24		$135

	Scale	LE	Value
❑			
❑			
❑			
❑			

Note: *Tony Stewart set a record in his rookie year by winning three races.*

How Many: Total Value:

Page Totals:	How Many	Total Value

Future Releases

Check our web site, *CollectorsQuest.com*, for new Tony Stewart product releases and record the information here.

Tony Stewart®	Value	How Many	Total Value

Page Totals:	How Many	Total Value

Future Releases

Check our web site, ***CollectorsQuest.com***, for new Tony Stewart product releases and record the information here.

Tony Stewart®	Value	How Many	Total Value

Page Totals:	How Many	Total Value

COLLECTOR'S VALUE GUIDE™

Rusty Wallace®

Rusty Wallace, a longtime favorite on the Winston Cup scene, has an extensive list of paint schemes under his belt. His "Adventures of Rusty" car was a hit with fans, while the Elvis paint scheme he ran at Las Vegas in 1998 appealed to Elvis fans and die-cast collectors alike. When not running a special promotional scheme, Wallace can be found in cars promoting Miller beer, his chief sponsor. Wallace has also run cars commemorating wins at the Texas Motor Speedway and the "Last Lap Of The Century."

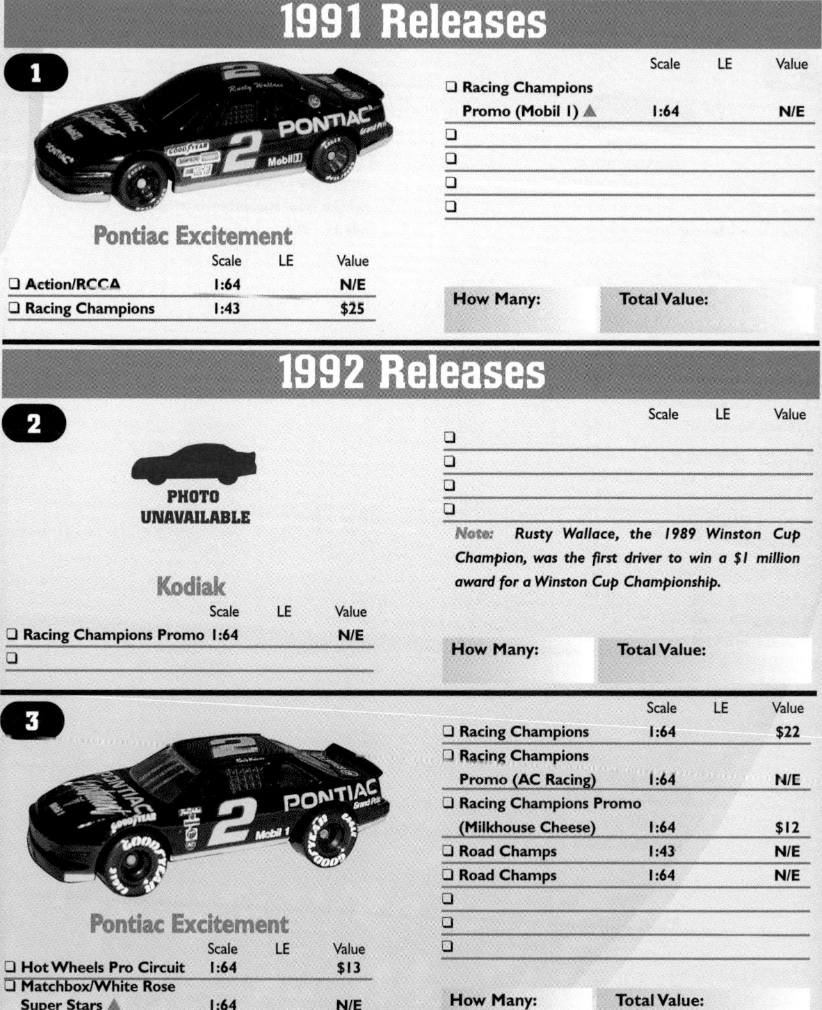

1991 Releases

1

Pontiac Excitement

	Scale	LE	Value
❑ Action/RCCA	1:64		N/E
❑ Racing Champions	1:43		$25

	Scale	LE	Value
❑ Racing Champions Promo (Mobil 1) ▲	1:64		N/E
❑			
❑			
❑			
❑			

How Many: | Total Value:

1992 Releases

2

PHOTO UNAVAILABLE

Kodiak

	Scale	LE	Value
❑ Racing Champions Promo	1:64		N/E
❑			

	Scale	LE	Value
❑			
❑			
❑			
❑			

Note: Rusty Wallace, the 1989 Winston Cup Champion, was the first driver to win a $1 million award for a Winston Cup Championship.

How Many: | Total Value:

3

Pontiac Excitement

	Scale	LE	Value
❑ Hot Wheels Pro Circuit	1:64		$13
❑ Matchbox/White Rose Super Stars ▲	1:64		N/E

	Scale	LE	Value
❑ Racing Champions	1:64		$22
❑ Racing Champions Promo (AC Racing)	1:64		N/E
❑ Racing Champions Promo (Milkhouse Cheese)	1:64		$12
❑ Road Champs	1:43		N/E
❑ Road Champs	1:64		N/E
❑			
❑			
❑			

How Many: | Total Value:

Page Totals:	How Many	Total Value

1993 Releases

Pontiac Excitement

	Scale	LE	Value
❑ Action/RCCA (AC Racing)	1:64		$25
❑ Action/RCCA (Delco Remy)	1:64		$35
❑ Racing Champions	1:43		$26
❑ Racing Champions	1:64		$19
❑ Racing Champions Premier	1:64		$26
❑ Racing Champions PVC Box Premier (Hot Just Got Hotter)	1:64		N/E

Note: *Due to a tangle with Dale Earnhardt, Wallace was airborne when he crossed the finish line at Talladega in 1993.*

How Many: Total Value:

1994 Releases

Ford Motorsports

	Scale	LE	Value
❑ Action	1:64		$14
❑ Action/RCCA	1:24		$260
❑ Matchbox/White Rose Super Stars	1:64		$12
❑ Racing Champions	1:24		N/E
❑ Racing Champions (black Ford oval)	1:24		N/E
❑ Racing Champions	1:64		$16
❑ Racing Champions (yellow box)	1:64		N/E
❑ Racing Champions Premier	1:43		$36
❑ Racing Champions Premier	1:64		$32
❑ Racing Champions To The MAXX	1:64		$27
❑			
❑			
❑			
❑			

Note: *Rusty Wallace won the first Winston Cup race held at New Hampshire International Speedway on July 11, 1993.*

How Many: Total Value:

6

Mac Tools

	Scale	LE	Value
❑ Racing Champions Premier	1:64		$35
❑			
❑			
❑			
❑			

How Many: Total Value:

Page Totals:	How Many	Total Value

1995 Releases

7

Ford Motorsports

	Scale	LE	Value
❑ Action/RCCA	1:24		$260
❑ Racing Champions	1:24		N/E
❑ Racing Champions	1:64		$14
❑ Racing Champions Matched Serial Numbers	1:64		$18
❑ Racing Champions Premier	1:64		$19
❑ Racing Champions Preview	1:24		$49
❑ Racing Champions Preview	1:64		$17
❑ Racing Champions To The MAXX	1:64		N/E
❑			
❑			

How Many: Total Value:

8

Kodiak

	Scale	LE	Value
❑ Action/RCCA ▲	1:24		$300
❑ Action/RCCA	1:64		$85
❑			
❑			
❑			
❑			

Note: Rusty Wallace hosted Win!, a weekly racing program broadcast on TNN.

How Many: Total Value:

9

Miller Genuine Draft

	Scale	LE	Value
❑ Action	1:24		N/E
❑ Action	1:64		$33
❑ Action (hood open)	1:64		N/E
❑ Action/RCCA	1:64		$35
❑ Ertl	1:18		$150
❑			
❑			
❑			
❑			

How Many: Total Value:

1996 Releases

10

Kodiak

	Scale	LE	Value
❑ Action	1:24		N/E
❑ Action	1:64		N/E
❑ Action/RCCA ▲	1:24		$290
❑ Action/RCCA	1:64		$65
❑ Ertl	1:18		$83
❑			
❑			

Note: On June 12, 1988, Rusty Wallace won the last Winston Cup race held at California's Ontario Motor Speedway.

How Many: Total Value:

Page Totals:	How Many	Total Value

11

Miller

	Scale	LE	Value
❑ Action	1:24		$130
❑ Action	1:64		$23
❑ Action/RCCA	1:24		N/E
❑ Action/RCCA	1:64		$52
❑ Matchbox/White Rose Super Stars Promo	1:64		$100
❑ Racing Champions	1:18		$70
❑ Racing Champions	1:24		$50
❑ Racing Champions (hood open)	1:24		$76
❑ Racing Champions	1:64		$24
❑ Racing Champions Premier with emblem	1:64		$25
❑ Racing Champions Promo	1:24		$65
❑ Revell Collection	1:24		$85
❑ Revell Collection	1:64		$28
❑ Revell Collection (Suzuka Thunder) ▲	1:64		$80
❑			
❑			
❑			
❑			

Note: *Wallace is a talented racer in all venues, but performs especially well on short tracks.*

How Many: | Total Value:

12

Miller

	Scale	LE	Value
❑ Racing Champions Chrome Chase ▲	1:64		N/E
❑			
❑			
❑			
❑			

How Many: | Total Value:

13

Miller Genuine Draft (Grand Prix)

	Scale	LE	Value
❑ Ertl	1:18		$85
❑			
❑			
❑			
❑			
❑			

Note: *Wallace won at Watkins Glen in 1987, even though he had to make a pit stop in his final lap.*

How Many: | Total Value:

Page Totals:	How Many	Total Value

14

PHOTO UNAVAILABLE

Miller Genuine Draft (Thunderbird)

	Scale	LE	Value
❑ Ertl	1:18		$90
❑			
❑			
❑			
❑			
❑			

Note: Through 1999, Wallace has finished in the top-ten point standings for seven consecutive seasons.

How Many: | Total Value:

15

Miller Silver Anniversary

	Scale	LE	Value
❑ Action ▲	1:24		$120
❑ Action	1:64		$28
❑ Action/RCCA	1:24		$120
❑ Action/RCCA	1:64		$60
❑ Ertl	1:18		$82
❑ Revell	1:24		$45
❑ Revell	1:64		$18
❑ Revell Collection	1:24		$90
❑ Revell Collection	1:64		$32
❑			
❑			
❑			

How Many: | Total Value:

16

Penske Racing

	Scale	LE	Value
❑ Racing Champions ▲	1:24		$48
❑ Racing Champions	1:64		$12
❑ Racing Champions Premier with emblem	1:64		N/E
❑ Revell	1:24		$25
❑ Revell	1:64		$16
❑			
❑			
❑			
❑			

How Many: | Total Value:

17

Penske Racing

	Scale	LE	Value
❑ Racing Champions Chrome Chase ▲	1:64		$225
❑			
❑			
❑			
❑			

Note: Rusty Wallace led his first race lap in 1984, at Darlington in the TranSouth 500.

How Many: | Total Value:

Page Totals:	How Many	Total Value

1997 Releases

18

Miller

	Scale	LE	Value
❑ Action	1:24		$79
❑ Action	1:64		$24
❑ Action/RCCA	1:64		$28
❑ Action/RCCA Elite ▲	1:24		$115
❑ Revell Collection	1:24		$83
❑			
❑			
❑			

Note: In November of 1996, Rusty Wallace won the first Suzuka Circuit race in Japan.

How Many:	Total Value:

19

Miller Genuine Draft

	Scale	LE	Value
❑ Action ▲	1:64		$33
❑ Action/RCCA	1:24		$175
❑			
❑			
❑			
❑			

Note: Rusty Wallace's first race win was on April 6, 1986 at Bristol International Raceway in the Valleydale 500.

How Many:	Total Value:

20

Miller Lite

	Scale	LE	Value
❑ Action	1:24		$86
❑ Action	1:64		$19
❑ Action (Texas)	1:64		$23
❑ Action/RCCA (Texas)	1:24		$90
❑ Action/RCCA	1:64		$30
❑ Action/RCCA (Texas)	1:64		$42
❑ Action/RCCA Elite ▲	1:24		$160
❑ Action/RCCA Elite (Texas)	1:24		$150
❑ Matchbox/White Rose Super Stars Promo	1:64		$80
❑ Revell Club	1:24		$95
❑ Revell Club (Texas)	1:24		N/E
❑ Revell Collection	1:18		$104
❑ Revell Collection	1:24		$75
❑ Revell Collection (Texas)	1:24		$85
❑ Revell Collection	1:43		$42
❑ Revell Collection	1:64		$24
❑ Revell Collection (Texas)	1:64		$25
❑ Revell Select	1:24		$44
❑ Revell Select	1:64		$20
❑			
❑			
❑			
❑			

How Many:	Total Value:

Page Totals:	How Many	Total Value

21

PHOTO UNAVAILABLE

Miller Lite

	Scale	LE	Value
❑ Racing Champions Chrome Chase (Matco Tool)	1:24		N/E

	Scale	LE	Value
❑			
❑			
❑			
❑			

Note: In 1997, Rusty Wallace was black-flagged during the Hanes 500 and used profanity when discussing the incident during post-race interviews. NASCAR fined him $5,000 for the offense and he paid the fine with 500,000 pennies delivered to Bill France in an armored truck.

How Many: **Total Value:**

22

Miller Lite

	Scale	LE	Value
❑ Racing Champions Gold	1:18		$195
❑ Racing Champions Gold ▲	1:24		N/E

	Scale	LE	Value
❑ Racing Champions Gold	1:64		$32
❑ Racing Champions Gold Chrome	1:18		$380
❑ Racing Champions Gold Chrome	1:64		$175
❑			
❑			
❑			

Note: Rusty Wallace's 1988 win at Rockingham came despite his having to make up a three-lap deficit.

How Many: **Total Value:**

23

Penske Racing

	Scale	LE	Value
❑ Racing Champions ▲	1:24		$34
❑ Racing Champions	1:64		$12

	Scale	LE	Value
❑ Racing Champions	1:144		$6
❑ Racing Champions Premier with emblem	1:64		$16
❑ Racing Champions Preview	1:64		N/E
❑ Racing Champions Roaring Racers	1:64		N/E
❑ Revell	1:24		$40
❑ Revell	1:64		$14
❑			

How Many: **Total Value:**

Page Totals:	How Many	Total Value

1998 Releases

24

Adventures Of Rusty

	Scale	LE	Value
❑ Action	1:24		$70
❑ Action	1:64		$20
❑ Action/RCCA	1:64		$26
❑ Action/RCCA Elite	1:24		$143
❑ Revell Club	1:18		$195
❑ Revell Club	1:24		$162
❑ Revell Collection	1:18		$95
❑ Revell Collection ▲	1:24		$66
❑ Revell Collection	1:43		$33
❑ Revell Collection	1:64		$18
❑ Revell Select	1:24		$39
❑ Revell Select	1:64		$15
❑ Winner's Circle	1:64		N/E
❑			
❑			
❑			
❑			
❑			
❑			
❑			

Note: Rusty Wallace is an accomplished pilot who owns three airplanes.

How Many: Total Value:

25

Elvis

	Scale	LE	Value
❑ Action	1:24		$72
❑ Action	1:64		$22
❑ Action/RCCA	1:64		$28
❑ Action/RCCA Elite	1:24		$138
❑ Revell Club	1:18		$142
❑ Revell Club	1:24		$110
❑ Revell Collection	1:18		$100
❑ Revell Collection ▲	1:24		$68
❑ Revell Collection	1:43		$38
❑ Revell Collection	1:64		$18
❑ Revell Select	1:24		$47
❑ Winner's Circle	1:24		$32
❑ Winner's Circle	1:43		N/E
❑ Winner's Circle	1:64		N/E
❑			
❑			

How Many: Total Value:

26

Gatorade

	Scale	LE	Value
❑ Johnny Lightning Stock Car Legends ▲	1:64		$17
❑			
❑			
❑			
❑			

Note: Rusty Wallace was the 1984 Winston Cup Rookie Of The Year.

How Many: Total Value:

Page Totals:	How Many	Total Value

27

Miller Lite

	Scale	LE	Value
❑ Action ▲	1:24		$76
❑ Action	1:64		$20

	Scale	LE	Value
❑ Action Promo (Ford Catalog)	1:32		N/E
❑ Action/RCCA	1:64		$24
❑ Action/RCCA Elite	1:24		$150
❑ Revell Club	1:24		$140
❑ Revell Collection	1:18		$95
❑ Revell Collection	1:24		$73
❑ Revell Collection	1:64		$15
❑ Revell Select	1:24		$40
❑ Revell Select	1:64		$14
❑			

How Many: **Total Value:**

28

PHOTO UNAVAILABLE

Miller Lite

	Scale	LE	Value
❑ Action/RCCA Gold	1:32		$80
❑			

	Scale	LE	Value
❑			
❑			
❑			
❑			

Note: *Wallace was named the 1991 IROC champion, after a successful year which included wins at Talladega, Michigan and Watkins Glen.*

How Many: **Total Value:**

29

Rusty

	Scale	LE	Value
❑ Winner's Circle	1:43		N/E
❑ Winner's Circle ▲	1:64		$10

	Scale	LE	Value
❑			
❑			
❑			
❑			

Note: *Rusty Wallace named some of his race cars "Madonna" and "Whitney" in honor of the singers.*

How Many: **Total Value:**

30

Taking Care Of Business

	Scale	LE	Value
❑ Action	1:24		$62
❑ Action	1:64		$20

	Scale	LE	Value
❑ Action/RCCA	1:64		$25
❑ Action/RCCA Elite	1:24		$120
❑ Revell Collection	1:18		$97
❑ Revell Collection ▲	1:24		$65
❑ Revell Collection	1:43		$38
❑ Revell Collection	1:64		$18
❑ Revell Select	1:24		$42
❑			
❑			
❑			

How Many: **Total Value:**

Page Totals:	How Many	Total Value

1999 Releases

31

Harley-Davidson

	Scale	LE	Value
❑ Action	1:18		$92
❑ Action	1:24		$80
❑ Action	1:64		$21
❑ Action/RCCA	1:64		$26
❑ Action/RCCA Elite	1:24		$255
❑ Revell Club	1:24		$125
❑ Revell Collection ▲	1:24		$82
❑ Revell Collection	1:43		$35
❑ Revell Collection	1:64		$22
❑			

How Many: Total Value:

32

Miller Lite

	Scale	LE	Value
❑ Action	1:18		$88
❑ Action	1:24		$72
❑ Action (Last Lap)	1:24		$79
❑ Action (True to Texas)	1:24		$80
❑ Action	1:64		$18
❑ Action (Last Lap)	1:64		$21
❑ Action (True to Texas)	1:64		$16
❑ Action/RCCA	1:64		$22
❑ Action/RCCA (Last Lap)	1:64		$29
❑ Action/RCCA (True to Texas)	1:64		$21
❑ Action/RCCA Elite	1:24		$165
❑ Action/RCCA Elite (Last Lap) ▲	1:24		$185
❑ Revell Club	1:18		$120
❑ Revell Club	1:24		$100
❑ Revell Collection	1:18		$85
❑ Revell Collection	1:24		$65
❑ Revell Collection	1:64		$16
❑			
❑			
❑			
❑			

Note: *Rusty Wallace won his first pole position on June 26, 1987 at Michigan in the Miller 400.*

How Many: Total Value:

33

Rusty

	Scale	LE	Value
❑ Winner's Circle ▲	1:24		$22
❑ Winner's Circle	1:64		$8
❑ Winner's Circle Speedweeks Series	1:64		$9
❑ Winner's Circle Tech Series	1:64		$9
❑			
❑			
❑			
❑			

How Many: Total Value:

Page Totals:	How Many	Total Value

2000 Releases

34

Harley-Davidson

	Scale	LE	Value
❑ Action/RCCA	1:64		$22
❑ Action/RCCA Elite ▲	1:24		$170
❑ Action/RCCA TotalView	1:64		$28
❑ Revell Club	1:24		$110
❑ Revell Collection	1:24		$72
❑			
❑			
❑			
❑			

How Many: | Total Value:

35

Miller Lite

	Scale	LE	Value
❑ Action ▲	1:24		$63
❑ Action	1:64		$16
❑ Action/RCCA	1:64		$20
❑ Action/RCCA Elite	1:24		$150
❑			
❑			
❑			
❑			

How Many: | Total Value:

36

PHOTO UNAVAILABLE

Miller Lite

	Scale	LE	Value
❑ Action 24K Gold (QVC Exclusive)	1:24		N/E
❑			
❑			
❑			
❑			

How Many: | Total Value:

37

PHOTO UNAVAILABLE

Rusty

	Scale	LE	Value
❑ Winner's Circle Sneak Preview Series	1:64		N/E
❑			
❑			
❑			
❑			

How Many: | Total Value:

Page Totals:	How Many	Total Value

Future Releases

Check our web site, ***CollectorsQuest.com***, for new Rusty Wallace product releases and record the information here.

Rusty Wallace®	Value	How Many	Total Value

Page Totals:	How Many	Total Value

Total Value Of My Collection

Record your collection here by adding the totals from the bottom of each Value Guide page.

Jeff Burton

Page Number	How Many	Total Value
Page 65		
Page 66		
Page 67		
Page 68		
Page 69		
Page 70		
Page 71		
Page 72		
Page 73		
Page 74		
Page 75		
Page 76		
Subtotal		

Dale Earnhardt®

Page Number	How Many	Total Value
Page 77		
Page 78		
Page 79		
Page 80		
Page 81		
Page 82		
Page 83		
Page 84		
Page 85		
Page 86		
Page 87		
Page 88		
Subtotal		

Page Totals:	How Many	Total Value

Total Value Of My Collection

Record your collection here by adding the totals from the bottom of each Value Guide page.

Dale Earnhardt®, cont.		
Page Number	How Many	Total Value
Page 89		
Page 90		
Page 91		
Page 92		
Page 93		
Page 94		
Page 95		
Page 96		
Page 97		
Page 98		
Page 99		
Page 100		
Page 101		
Page 102		
Subtotal		

Dale Earnhardt®, cont.		
Page Number	How Many	Total Value
Page 103		
Page 104		
Page 105		
Page 106		
Dale Earnhardt Jr.		
Page 107		
Page 108		
Page 109		
Page 110		
Page 111		
Page 112		
Page 113		
Page 114		
Page 115		
Subtotal		

Page Totals:	How Many	Total Value

COLLECTOR'S VALUE GUIDE™

Total Value Of My Collection

Record your collection here by adding the totals from the bottom of each Value Guide page.

Jeff Gordon®

Page Number	How Many	Total Value
Page 116		
Page 117		
Page 118		
Page 119		
Page 120		
Page 121		
Page 122		
Page 123		
Page 124		
Page 125		
Page 126		
Page 127		
Subtotal		

Jeff Gordon®, cont.

Page Number	How Many	Total Value
Page 128		

Dale Jarrett®

Page Number	How Many	Total Value
Page 129		
Page 130		
Page 131		
Page 132		
Page 133		
Page 134		
Page 135		
Page 136		
Page 137		
Page 138		
Subtotal		

Page Totals:	How Many	Total Value

Total Value Of My Collection

Record your collection here by adding the totals from the bottom of each Value Guide page.

Bobby Labonte™		
Page Number	How Many	Total Value
Page 139		
Page 140		
Page 141		
Page 142		
Page 143		
Page 144		
Page 145		
Page 146		
Page 147		
Page 148		
Mark Martin®		
Page 149		
Page 150		
Subtotal		

Mark Martin®, cont.		
Page Number	How Many	Total Value
Page 151		
Page 152		
Page 153		
Page 154		
Page 155		
Page 156		
Page 157		
Page 158		
Page 159		
Page 160		
Page 161		
Page 162		
Page 163		
Subtotal		

Page Totals:	How Many	Total Value

COLLECTOR'S VALUE GUIDE™

Total Value Of My Collection

Record your collection here by adding the totals from the bottom of each Value Guide page.

Mark Martin®, cont.

Page Number	How Many	Total Value
Page 164		
Page 165		
Page 166		
Page 167		
Page 168		

Tony Stewart®

Page Number	How Many	Total Value
Page 169		
Page 170		
Page 171		
Page 172		
Page 173		
Page 174		
Subtotal		

Rusty Wallace®

Page Number	How Many	Total Value
Page 175		
Page 176		
Page 177		
Page 178		
Page 179		
Page 180		
Page 181		
Page 182		
Page 183		
Page 184		
Page 185		
Page 186		
Subtotal		

Grand Total:	How Many	Total Value

Die-Cast Overview

Die-cast replicas of cars have been around almost as long as the real ones, but today, thanks in part to the popularity of NASCAR, there are more die-cast collectibles available than ever before.

The Beginning

For many years, die-cast cars were available from companies such as as Matchbox® and Hot Wheels®. In the beginning, however, the companies did not produce NASCAR die-cast as we know it today. Instead, they produced models of fantasy and classic cars and threw in the occasional NASCAR-themed model. The modern era of NASCAR die-cast, with replicas made of almost every car raced, did not start until Racing Champions® was founded and innovated its unique approach to NASCAR die-cast: instead of producing an occasional NASCAR die-cast in a line of general models, Racing Champions would make NASCAR die-cast its focus.

One of the first collectibles companies to take part in NASCAR's licensing and merchandising program, Racing Champions started the die-cast craze in 1989 with a series of cars now known as "flat-bottom," named after the flat-bottomed blister packs in which the cars were sold. The flat-bottom series contained only six cars, featuring notable drivers of the time: Bill Elliott, Dale Earnhardt, Davey Allison, Larry Pearson, Michael Waltrip and Sterling Marlin. In 1990, Racing Champions expanded its roster of

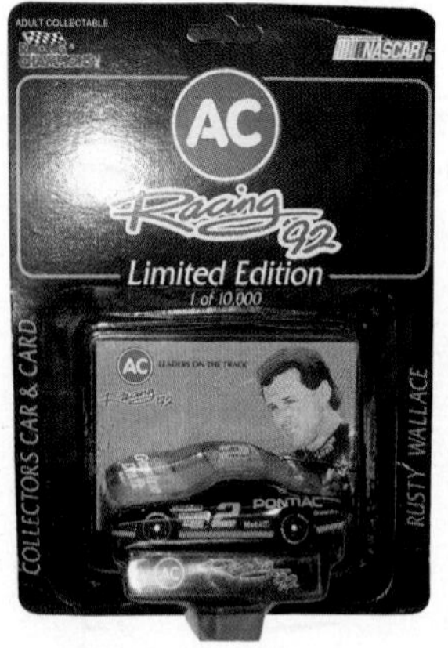

models and began packaging its products in a bubble-bottom package. The bubble-bottom, which is used today, raises the car enough to make it clearly visible from inside the box. It was then that the modern era of NASCAR die-cast was born.

Racing Champions was founded by Boyd Meyer and Bob Dods, two entrepreneurs whose approach to die-cast manufacturing was doubly innovative; not only were they the first to focus solely on NASCAR die-cast, but they were among the pioneers of distributing NASCAR products through the retail market rather than exclusively through trackside or hobby-store outlets. The increased availability of NASCAR products naturally led to greater exposure for the sport itself and NASCAR die-cast collectibles might not enjoy the popularity they do today if not for Meyer and Dods.

Movie Mania

Other die-cast historians credit the modern popularity of die-cast to the 1990 movie *Days of Thunder*. While other films based on legendary NASCAR drivers have been released in the past, none were as big at the box office as *Days of Thunder*, starring film icon Tom Cruise. The success of the film led to mass production of die-cast pieces based on the cars seen in the movie and even after the initial hype for the movie had died down, die-cast replicas of NASCAR cars remained popular.

Whether started by Racing Champions or *Days of Thunder*, by 1994 the NASCAR die-cast hobby was already showing signs of the huge popularity it would enjoy today. In fact, by the mid-1990s many of the die-cast companies we're now familiar with were putting out a full selection of NASCAR die-cast each year.

Another major die-cast manufacturer to make a name for itself around this time was Action Performance Companies Inc.®, whose president Fred Wagenhals began the company in 1992. One of his first moves was to buy the Racing Collectibles Club of America® (RCCA) and Racing Collectibles Incorporated (RCI). In 1993, Wagenhals signed a licensing contract with Dale Earnhardt, and took the company public.

It was Wagenhals who started the modern NASCAR paint-scheme craze in 1995, when he convinced Dale Earnhardt to run his special one-time silver paint scheme in the 1995 Winston. The idea was the single most successful die-cast marketing program in history, as subsequent sales of die-cast models of the car skyrocketed and the NASCAR paint-scheme mania of today was born. 1995 was also the first year a paint scheme was used to promote a movie, with Bill Elliott's popular "Thunderbat" car created in anticipation of the film *Batman Forever*.

Wagenhals and Action inspired many other movie tie-ins (a tradition which continues today) such as the *Small Soldiers* movie promotion by Tony Stewart and Bobby Labonte and the "Batman" and "Joker" cars driven by Dale Jarrett and Kenny Irwin. But perhaps this connection between using movies to promote products and products to promote movies was a natural one for Wagenhals, since he had connections to the movie industry ever since he invented the motor that powered the mechanical bull first seen in John Travolta's movie *Urban Cowboy*.

While Racing Champions and Action are two of the biggest names in the die-cast industry, there are many smaller companies whose products are also highly respected. Ertl® is one of the oldest die-cast collectible manufacturers in the industry, while the Brookfield Collectors Guild™ has a firm reputation as a producer of high-quality, limited-edition collectibles. These days, though, most of the smaller companies no longer exist, or exist as subsidiaries of the well-known manufacturing giants. Ertl, for example, was bought out by Racing Champions, while Action bought Revell™, Brookfield Collectors Guild, Racing Collectibles Club of America and several other respected names in the die-cast industry. Team Caliber™ is one of the newest die-cast companies around and while their production runs are small, their cars are known to be of high quality.

The Rest Of The Bunch

Cars are the best-known of the die-cast models, although there are several other types of products available, both NASCAR-related and otherwise. NASCAR collectors can flesh out their die-cast car collections with the addition of die-cast transporters, pit wagons and even airplanes, all decorated with their favorite driver's numbers and color schemes. Action also makes 1:43 scale reproductions of children's pedal cars, with movable pedals and working steering wheels. Each car is decorated in a different paint scheme of a popular NASCAR driver.

Banks decorated in NASCAR paint schemes are another popular subcategory of die-cast. Action, for example, makes 1:24 scale car banks that are virtually indistinguishable from its 1:24 scale cars, except that the banks sometimes have black windows rather than clear and all contain a coin slot in the back window. Most die-cast pit wagons and airplanes come in bank form, also. Some die-cast collectors even choose to concentrate on banks rather than cars.

There's plenty of non-NASCAR and even non-racing die-cast, as well, though they're not as prevalent as they were in the days before the NASCAR craze took hold. Racing Champions makes racing-related die-cast dragsters, funny cars and Indy racers, and John Deere® has for a long time made die-cast models of its tractors and other farm equipment.

How It's Done

The phrase "die-cast" is derived from "die casting," a metalworking process that involves forcing molten metal into a special mold called a die. Once the metal re-solidifies and cools, the result is also called a die casting. The process is a lot more complicated than it sounds, though, especially for those die castings destined to become NASCAR die-cast models.

Before work on a NASCAR die-cast car even begins, there are a number of legal matters that must be settled. Every sponsor whose name is on the car must be contacted, royalty agreements must be hammered out and numerous contracts must be signed.

Once permissions have been secured, the car is carefully researched and photographed from every angle so the die-cast designer will know what the car looks like. When the design has been finalized, the artwork is sent off to factories which are often located overseas. A clay prototype of the car is carefully constructed, followed by a lot of back-and-forth discussions and adjustments, all before the actual die casting can begin.

A die mold, also known as a "tool," is then made of high-quality steel. The tool is usually made of eight sliding pieces that form a hollow space in the shape of a die-cast car. Molten zinc alloy is injected into these spaces and when the metal cools and solidifies, the tool is pulled apart, allowing the die-casting to fall out.

Each piece is then filed by hand, machine-polished and carefully cleaned before the paint and graphics can be added. The painting process for die-cast cars is not unlike that of real ones, with primer and paint being baked onto the metal.

To add the sponsor names on the car, tampo printing, a painting process similar to rubber-stamping, has replaced the traditional method of adhering decals to the side. Next, the smaller pieces of the car, such as the windows, wheels and interior parts, are attached. Finally, the completed products are shipped to stores so that they can end up in some lucky fan's collection.

Keep Reading

For more information on the die-cast production process, turn to page 228 to view our section on "The Making Of A Die-Cast Collectible."

Secondary Market Overview

It's amazing to think that just a little over ten years ago, a die-cast car that now sells for over a hundred dollars, could then be had for at retail for just a few dollars. Nowadays, of course, you can't find the older die-cast cars in virtually any retail store. So does that mean you can never add these pieces to your own collection? No, it just means you'll have to check out the secondary market.

What Is It?

The secondary market is made up of collectors who buy, sell or trade various items, while the primary market consists of retail stores, hobby outlets or home shopping channels. So, you may wonder, why would you need to go to the secondary market if pieces are available through retail stores?

> ***Secondary Market Terms***
>
> **damaged box (DB)** – a secondary market term used when a collectible's box is in poor condition, oftentimes diminishing the value of the item.
>
> **mint in box (MIB)** – a secondary market term used when a collectible's original box is "good as new," which usually adds to the value of the item.
>
> **no box (NB)** – a secondary market term used when a collectible's original box is missing. For most collectibles, having the original box is a factor in the value.

In most cases, a collector will pursue a piece on the secondary market when they have exhausted all the retailers and are still unable to find what they are looking for. In the die-cast collectibles market, most pieces are available as limited editions, so once the stock has been depleted, collectors who missed out on the opportunity will move to other resources, even though the piece may have now significantly increased in value.

Shopping The Secondary Market

There is no "secondary market" listing in the Yellow Pages, so where do you go to find it? It used to be confined to collectibles stores, flea markets, classified ads and the occasional swap meet and prices were high and varied from place to place. Since it was hard for buyers to find certain pieces, it was very much a seller's market and the sellers usually had more say than the buyers in determining what a price would be. The Internet has changed all that, however. Suddenly buyers are no longer confined to choosing from those few outlets available in their area. Instead, a click or two of the mouse brings potential sellers in contact with potential buyers all over the country or even the world.

The Internet has helped the sellers, too. In fact, in recent years, the number of potential customers has skyrocketed. Internet stores and auctions have created a secondary market far larger than anything seen in the history of the industry. For more information on the secondary market and the Internet, check out the "NASCAR On The Net" section later in the book.

Getting The Best Price

The most important factor in determining a particular item's secondary market value is its condition. Most price guide listings are for items in mint condition and flaws in the quality of the items such as scratches in the paint or decals that have worn off, can unfortunately reduce the value of your NASCAR die-cast by a significant percentage. That's why it's so important for you to take good care of your collectibles.

Box It Up!

It is also important that the die-cast items remain in their original boxes. Many die-cast manufacturers currently package their cars so that they can be displayed while still in the box, but that wasn't the case in the early days and so the older a car is, the harder it may be to find in its box. Most price guide listings assume the cars are still in their boxes and for a piece that is missing its box, or if the box is in bad condition, the value can be cut significantly.

Boxes are not so important when dealing with collectible plastic models, however. In fact, collectors of NASCAR model kits are more concerned that all the parts are there and are in good shape, than whether or not the box is in pristine condition. Some model-kit collectors actually prefer models in the opened boxes, so that they can check inside to make sure that all the parts are in good condition and accounted for. For cereal-box collectors, meanwhile, the boxes can be opened up, unfolded and broken down, just so long as the panels on the boxes are not folded or creased.

Don't Be Swayed

When buying on the secondary market, remember that you ultimately set the price. You know how much a particular item is worth to you and you should always be certain not to let anyone pressure you into paying more than that.

Retirements

Many of the rules that apply to the secondary market for other lines of collectibles do not stand up in the world of NASCAR die-cast collecting. For example, most other lines of contemporary collectibles tend to be produced for specific periods of time, which can range from months to years and when they are no longer produced, they are said to be "retired."

This doesn't apply to NASCAR die-cast collecting. On the one hand, new die-cast models are produced every year, which means last year's cars can be said to have retired; on the other hand, companies have not set their production schedules in stone and so a particularly well-selling car may be sold even after its official year is over. Also, production numbers are not always precise: a car might be labeled as "one of 10,000," when in reality, the manufacturer made far more or less than that number.

No Autographs, Please

You'd think that a die-cast Jeff Gordon car would be worth more money if Jeff Gordon signed it, right? Not necessarily. For some collectors, the autograph will increase the value of the car, but many die-cast collectors are purists who feel the autograph decreases the value of the model, since the original race car was not autographed when it ran in

races. It is up to you, the collector, to decide how much an autographed car is worth to you; but as a seller trying to get the highest possible price you're better off leaving your cars as is, rather than trying to get them autographed.

Things To Remember

Whether buying or selling NASCAR die-cast on the secondary market, always try to remember that prices vary from month to month and even day to day. If an item is too expensive for you to buy right now, or selling more cheaply than you as a seller want to accept, consider trying again in a couple of months and see if the price isn't more to your liking. And always remember: buy collectibles because you enjoy them, not for their perceived investment potential. That way, no matter what happens to the secondary market value of your NASCAR collectibles, you'll still be happy with your purchase.

Insuring Your Collection

Now that you've devoted a lot of time, effort and money building up your collection of NASCAR collectibles, make sure that your collection is covered in the event of theft, flood, fire or other unforeseen circumstances. Insuring your collection is a wise move and it does not have to be costly or difficult.

1. Assess the value of your collection. If it is quite extensive, you might want to have it professionally appraised. However, you can determine the current value of your collection yourself by checking a reputable price guide such as the Collector's Value Guide™.

2. Determine the amount of coverage you need. Collectibles are often covered under a basic homeowner's or renter's policy, but ask your agent if your policy covers fire, theft, flood, hurricanes, earthquakes and damage or breakage from routine handling. Also, find out if your policy covers claims at "current replacement value" – the amount it would cost to replace items if they were damaged, lost or stolen. If the amount of insurance does not cover your collection, you may want to consider adding a Personal Articles Floater or a Fine Arts Floater ("rider") to your policy. Many insurance companies specialize in collectibles insurance and can help you ensure that your collection is adequately covered.

3. Keep up-to-date documentation of your collectible pieces and their values. Save all your receipts and consider photographing each item, taking special care to show color changes, signatures and other special features in the photograph. Keep all of your documentation in a safe place, such as a safe deposit box, or make two copies and give one to a friend or relative.

Caring For Your Collection

Collecting die-cast cars is a thrilling hobby and NASCAR die-cast offers collectors a chance to really spice up their collection, thanks to the large variety of products available. Avid collectors like to display their collections and often have a special room designated for them. Nevertheless, the important thing to remember in collecting is quality, not quantity. A properly maintained small collection will bring far more pleasure than a poorly maintained large one.

Your collection should be kept in an environment where there is not excessive exposure to damaging elements, especially if the cars are going to be taken out of their packaging. The first thing to avoid when displaying your collectibles is exposure to dust. Moisture is also damaging, so basements aren't ideal to house your collection. In addition to avoiding dust and moisture, excessive sunlight can often fade the color of pieces.

Most collectors like to keep their cars in the original packaging because it preserves the car and adds to its value; however, if you do decide to remove your cars from their packages, many manufacturers build special wooden and plastic display cases for die-cast cars. Regular book shelves are an alternative to these special cases and are very popular with collectors who want to show off their collection. If you

decide to leave the car in its original packaging, the simplest way to display cars in a blister pack is to thumb-tack the package to a bulletin board or a wall. Do not tack a new hole through the package, though; use the pre-existing hole manufacturers use to hang blister packs on a display rack.

While handling your cars, avoid touching them with your bare hands, because the oils from your skin will tarnish the metal over time. Decals are more easily damaged than metal; therefore, try not to touch them at all. Some collectors use cotton gloves to safely handle their collection and avoid damage.

Should your car still get dirty despite these precautions, the less water used to clean it, the better. You can use a soft toothbrush to clean the small crevices and the body, but keep the bristles away from the decals. Ordinary glass cleaner will help give your car a new shine, but don't use a large amount. The best way to bring a dull car to its original luster is to use the car wax that you would use on the car you drive. This is a tricky process and beginners should start with their less valuable pieces first and then build their way up to the more valuable ones.

If your car should get any scratches or chips, small ones can be removed with touch-up paint. Do not attempt to redo the paint job on a car unless you have had a lot of experience with painting die-cast. This is a very complicated process and, if not done properly, can cause more damage than it fixes. If you plan on eventually selling your collection, you should stay away from repainting your cars altogether, but keep careful note of what restorative steps you do take, so that you can inform potential buyers.

NASCAR® On The Net

The Internet should not be overlooked as an important tool for both collectors of NASCAR memorabilia and fans of the sport alike. Up-to-the-minute point standings and racing news, essays about the history and personalities of NASCAR, collectibles auctions and catalogs filled with great NASCAR novelties for sale – all this and more can be had with just a click of your mouse when you access NASCAR through the Internet.

For first time users of the Internet or those who are just learning about the sports' presence in the dot-com world, the first place to check out is *www.NASCAR.com*, the official web site of the motorsports organization. There you'll find a comprehensive guide to all that is NASCAR – historical and statistical information about the racetracks, drivers and cars, race schedules, fan club listings, contact information and, occasionally, live on-line chats with featured drivers. There you'll also find an extensive collectibles section that features collectibles news, a question-and-answer column and even an on-line store. With all that and more, you'll want to be sure that when accessing the Internet that you make *www.NASCAR.com* your first stop to gear up on all of the latest NASCAR news and information.

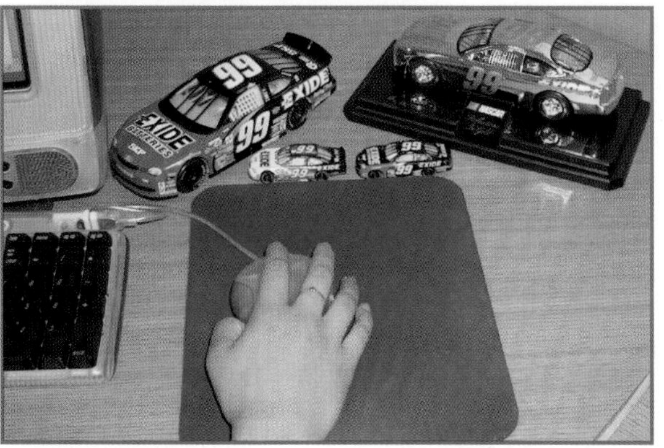

There are many other sites dedicated to NASCAR in particular or auto racing in general on the Internet, each of which is sure to provide you with a unique perspective on NASCAR racing. Many sites offer current news articles, dozens of essays about NASCAR history and chat rooms for talking to like-minded NASCAR fans. You can also find listings of scanner frequencies for the Winston Cup, Busch and Craftsman Truck series, allowing fans at the races to listen in as their favorite drivers converse with their pit crews. To locate web sites containing information about NASCAR and auto sports in general, try using one of the many available search engines on the net by combining the search term "NASCAR" with any of the variety of topics that are of particular interest to you. Plus, you can also check with your friends and family to see which NASCAR-related sites they rely on for the best coverage of the sport.

Another venue to check when hunting for NASCAR web sites is to take a look at the major television networks, both broadcast and cable, who all maintain a certain level of NASCAR awareness on their official web sites. The official web site of the ABC network (*www.abc.com*) works in conjunction with the exclusively-sports cable network ESPN (*www.espn.com*). Sports Illustrated magazine has combined forces with the Cable News Network for their web site, *www.CNNSI.com*, which contains NASCAR information under their "motor sports" link. TNN broadcasts many races, which can be heard, and even seen, through their web site at *www.tnnracing.com.*

In addition, there are plenty of web sites which are dedicated to specific NASCAR drivers. Most drivers maintain their own official web sites for their fans, so if you are looking to find firsthand information on your favorite racer, these sites are the place to look. Additionally, typing in NASCAR or any of the driver's names on any of the search engines can lead you to hundreds of unofficial web sites on each driver, most hosted by fans for fans to provide you with great, up-to-date information.

Buyer Beware

For every one web site featuring NASCAR information for free, there's at least one web site offering NASCAR merchandise for sale. Shopping on the Internet requires a few special precautions, however. Make sure to follow all of the usual precautions you would take when buying or paying for something by mail such as verifying who you are submitting your credit card number to. And you can even try to check with the Better Business Bureau before you purchase merchandise to see if a particular site has had any complaints lodged against it.

Even if a web-based business is legitimate, you should still take certain precautions. Always remember to never send your credit card number or any other personal information over the Internet unless you are sure that the web site is secure. Several web businesses feature Secure Socket Layer (SSL) protection, which encrypts your ordering.

CollectorsQuest.com

To keep yourself informed on the latest die-cast collecting news and information, try logging on to CheckerBee's own web site, located at ***www.CollectorsQuest.com.*** At **CollectorsQuest** you'll find all you need to know to keep yourself up-to-date on the die-cast market, as well as news and information on NASCAR racing.

information to ensure that unauthorized third parties can't get a look at it. If a web business is legitimate but its site is not secure, then pay for your purchases by mail and don't send any personal information when ordering on-line.

Going, Going, Gone!

Auctions are another popular Internet shopping option. Some on-line automotive or die-cast magazines feature auctions as a sideline and there are a variety of dedicated auction sites that allow collections to search for items to bid on and even place their own collections up for sale. In recent years, auctions have become yet another Internet phenomenon, so if don't already have some bookmarked on your computer, you can rely on your search engine to lead you directly to somc of the most popular ones on the net. Also, you can try scanning your Internet providers homepage, as many provide direct links to some of the biggest names in the industry.

When buying something from an on-line auctioneer, checking their credentials with the Better Business Bureau is unfortunately not an option. So how do you check a seller's credentials? Most auction sites allow users to issue "feedback," which enables buyers and sellers who have completed transactions to comment, either positively or negatively, upon their buying experience with the other party involved. So, if you're uncertain about whether or not to bid on an item that is up for auction, try to check the seller's feedback and see what others have had to say about their experience.

SOLD

A few auction sites on the Internet today also offer insurance to on-line buyers, although this practice is still not common. Even among those that do offer this option, there are limits to the coverage – for example, one site insures goods for up to $200 but there is a $25 deductible, which means that for items costing less than that, the insurance policy is of no use to a collector. For more information on how to safely utilize the variety of auctions on the Internet, you can check the site of the auction itself to see what buyer-protection policies are available.

Shopping for collectibles or researching information on the Internet is both easy and fun, but before you even think about going on-line, make sure your computer has a good virus-protection software program. Once you do have the anti-virus software set up, remember to update it regularly. Many viruses are spread via e-mail, so don't open e-mails or their attachments unless you know and trust the sender. Good luck!

Other Racing Collectibles

Fans of NASCAR may know that there are a wide variety of collectible items on the marketplace. However, if you're new to the sport, or new to the hobby of collecting sports memorabilia, you may be astonished by the scope of products you can find to buy, sell or trade on the secondary market. Here are just a few of the more popular collectible items that can be found in the marketplace today.

The Cars

While die-cast replicas, banks and models might be the best-known of the NASCAR collectibles, they are certainly not the only ones available to collectors today. In fact, the options for collectors who like die-cast cars alone are tremendous. In addition to the regular paint schemes, special event paint schemes, gold and chrome cars (which are highlighted in this book) there

Where To Begin

Confused about where to buy NASCAR collectibles? Aside from retailers, you can enhance your collection by shopping the secondary market. The secondary market can be a great source for buying and selling collectibles, though items are usually offered at a higher price than their original retail due to their limited availability. To locate pieces on the secondary market, you can contact local retailers to find a vendor in your area or you can search out dealers on the Internet who specialize in racing memorabilia. Another option is to try your hand at shopping the secondary market through an on-line auction site. For more information on the secondary market, turn to our "Secondary Market Overview" on page 198.

are a variety of additional products including crystal and pewter cars for automotive enthusiasts on the market today. Any store with a good die-cast selection probably carries a few of the pewter or crystal cars as well. However, these are not nearly as common as their die-cast cousins and many of the crystal and pewter models are only available as limited editions.

Also along the lines of the die-cast cars, and even rarer still than the pewter or crystal cars, are porcelain reproductions. Porcelain cars can be found in the 1:12 scale and are made by Integrity Collectibles. Adding to the mystique of porcelain cars is their extremely limited nature – Integrity Collectibles does not make more than 2,500 of each particular model.

The Drivers

But for some collectors this is not enough. Many NASCAR fans want a more personal piece of racing history, like a piece of the driver's car or uniform. While there are several types of these collectibles available (including fenders, hubcaps and pieces of scrap metal from the actual race cars), the most affordable of these types of collectibles are the used racing tires which, being relatively common, can be had for anywhere between $10 – $75 apiece. Keep in mind that they're usually cheaper when you buy them straight from the racetrack.

Other car parts are far pricier – an authenticated hood from Dale Earnhardt's car will easily sell for over $3,000, while hoods from other drivers commonly command prices of over $700. More expensive still than the hoods are the drivers' fire suits and racing helmets, which can sell for up to $5,000 or $6,000 apiece.

Not Just About Cars Anymore

As NASCAR has grown in popularity through the years, the number of officially licensed NASCAR collectibles has grown as well. One recent addition to the NASCAR collectibles lineup that is rapidly growing in popularity is the phone card. Supermarkets and convenience stores regularly sell long-distance phone cards and now you can find phone cards decorated with a picture of your favorite NASCAR driver, as well as their autograph. Phone cards are often no more expensive than their regular counterparts and you can usually find a used version selling for only a couple of dollars. Also, while searching for phone cards be sure to check out the ever-increasing line of collectible trading cards.

Time For NASCAR®

Clocks are also popular in the NASCAR collectibles market. Many companies produce clocks decorated with a driver's number, signature or likeness and all of the many brands of clocks on the market can often be found retailing for under $60. Also, like many of the other NASCAR collectibles, clocks have recently seen a rise in secondary market value and will often command prices of up to several hundred dollars.

The Cutting Edge

Knives are another popular subcategory of NASCAR collectibles, ranging from inexpensive single-blade pocketknives that fold out of a car-shaped handle to limited-edition bowie knives with walnut display cases that retail for close to a $1,000. These knives have a crossover appeal, both for

NASCAR fans and collectors of knives, which means they can be found not only in NASCAR stores and web sites but also in outlets that cater to knife collectors. The same holds true for collectible Zippo® lighters, which come in models commemorating both individual NASCAR drivers and specific races.

Rarities

While you can purchase collectible knives, cars, phone cards and the like through any number of stores and Internet sites, this isn't true for all NASCAR collectibles. Some collectibles are produced in extremely limited numbers, like the Dale Earnhardt Gibson guitars which were designed by Sam Bass, the automotive artist who designs many of the driver's paint schemes. His web site, *sambassart.com*, showcases up-and-coming paint schemes, as well as limited-edition NASCAR items for sale, such as lithographic prints and the Gibson guitars, of which only 333 were produced. Such extremely rare (and often expensive) items are more likely to be found commemorating the extremely popular drivers, which will often make finding a relatively new driver very difficult.

Supermarket Specials

Luckily, most NASCAR collectibles aren't as expensive or hard to find as the limited-edition Gibson guitars. You might already have a few collectibles in your kitchen! One popular NASCAR collectible is cereal boxes. Kellogg's® started the NASCAR collectible cereal trend in 1991, when it sponsored driver Larry Pearson and put a picture of his car on its Corn Flakes® box. Since then, Kellogg's has marketed over 60 different cereal boxes that have featured popular drivers such as Jeff Gordon, Terry Labonte and nearly a dozen others. General Mills® has also done NASCAR promotions, the best-known being the Dale Earnhardt Wheaties® boxes (which was especially collectible as he was the first NASCAR driver to appear on a Wheaties box). Additionally, Winn-Dixie has featured Mark Martin on some of its store-brand cereal boxes.

Knowledgeable cereal-box collectors say that it makes no difference to the value of a box if it is open or closed, full or empty; what really matters is that each panel of the box is smooth and uncreased. So if you're short on space (or worried about bugs) don't be afraid to open, empty and unfold your boxes; just make sure you don't bend them anywhere they weren't bent already.

NASCAR drivers have appeared on more than just cereal, too. In 1997, Close-Up® toothpaste ran a Jeff Gordon promotion that featured his picture on their toothpaste boxes and many beverage companies have run NASCAR promotions as well. So keep your eyes open the next time you go grocery shopping. Who knows what great, affordable collectibles you might find!

Happy Anniversary

In addition to the regularly marketed NASCAR collectibles, NASCAR's 50th anniversary in 1998 inspired a bonanza of commemorative collectible items. Anniversary versions of all the previously mentioned collectibles were unveiled for the banner year and fans could also buy such items as the NASCAR Barbie™ doll or USAOPOLY's NASCAR-themed Monopoly® board game featuring

popular drivers in place of the usual properties for sale (a Dale Earnhardt edition was also made). For book lovers, HarperCollins collaborated with NASCAR to publish the *NASCAR 50th Anniversary Book,* a beautifully illustrated history of America's most beloved sport.

Whether you are a die-hard NASCAR fan or just a part-time hobbyist, there is a wide variety of NASCAR collectibles to suit your desires. So whether your search takes you to your local track for that unique car part or to your local supermarket for a box of cereal, remember that half the fun is in the hunt for that perfect item! Good luck!

Racin' Up The Charts

After conquering TV and the movies, it was only a matter of time until NASCAR expanded into the music industry. Industry mogul Columbia Records has released two NASCAR-themed albums, "Hotter Than Asphalt" and "Running Wide Open," which NASCAR fans are sure to want to add to their music collections. Both feature country music by artists such as Waylon Jennings, Tanya Tucker, Hank Williams Jr. and Billy Ray Cyrus. Also, the country group Alabama has both a song and video entitled "Richard Petty Fans."

Other NASCAR® Products

In addition to NASCAR-themed collectibles, there are also many additional NASCAR products on the market. So you may wonder what the difference is between a collectible and a regular NASCAR product. It is important to remember that a collectible is something meant to increase in value over time and is, therefore, not often used for fear of marring its condition. Products, on the other hand, *are* intended for everyday use, and, while some of them have secondary market value, it is not always a guarantee that the value will go up. But they are a lot of fun and they let you show your support for your favorite driver!

Odds And Ends

Magazines, hobby shops and die-cast stores all offer selections of various NASCAR products, but for the greatest selection of unusual NASCAR novelties, your best bet is the Internet. Need a portable propane barbecue grill emblazoned with your favorite driver's insignia and shaped like a beer keg? Type "NASCAR Keg-a-Que" into a search engine and see how many web sites come up. (And shop around – prices can vary by as much as $30!) Want to bake a cake that's an exact replica of your favorite race car, complete with paint-scheme-colored icing and edible decals? Log on to *racecakes.com* and see if your favorite driver is available. Or perhaps you face hazardous conditions on the job? If so, then order yourself your favorite driver's number on a hard hat that's NASCAR-licensed and OSHA-approved.

NASCAR fans and golf lovers can log on the net to buy gift packs consisting of four golf balls, a divot tool and a ball marker, all with a specific driver's number and signature. Not a golf fan?

NASCAR-loving wine aficionados can contact Thoroughbred Vintners about their hand-etched and sequentially numbered wines made for both the 1999 Brickyard 400 and the 2000 Daytona 500. Fishermen, meanwhile, can contact Oxboro Outdoors™ to see their line of NASCAR-licensed lures.

Computer Games And Accessories

There are even NASCAR-themed computer games available. Most of these are racing-simulation games that let players recreate the feel of building and modifying the race car of their choice, developing its paint schemes and racing it on realistic reproductions of actual Winston Cup racetracks.

The computer company, Sierra, is credited with starting it all with their first NASCAR simulation software, *NASCAR Racing*. The game proved so popular with fans that it spawned two sequels, *NASCAR Racing 2* and *NASCAR Racing 3*, each one of which has become more realistic than its predecessor.

Sierra has also produced a NASCAR-licensed version of its popular 3D Ultra Pinball series for NASCAR enthusiasts. In *NASCAR 3D Ultra Pinball,* your position in the race depends upon how many points you score during the course of the game.

In addition to playing NASCAR games on your computer, you can also decorate it with NASCAR accessories. A mousepad with your favorite driver's picture on it is a good start and goes well with a mouse shaped like the driver's car. There are also NASCAR screensavers featuring all sorts of race-themed graphics. Some of these screensavers cost money, while others can be downloaded for free off of the Internet.

Clothes Make The Fan

Anyone who wants to can find enough NASCAR (or driver-themed) clothes and accessories to outfit themselves from head to toe. So if you're partial to dressing the part, you can surely find everything you need, from hats and caps, down to sneakers and everything else in between.

Dozens of companies produce t-shirts and sweatshirts with driver names and numbers on them and if it's a chilly day, a NASCAR coat or jacket can be added to the ensemble. Sweatpants are available for select drivers and those who want to can first put on a pair of NASCAR boxer shorts.

The shirts, pants and jackets are also readily available in women's sizes. And the women who wear them can also choose to accessorize their outfits with NASCAR-themed earrings, necklaces and hair scrunchies.

For NASCAR families who don't want to overlook the smallest fans in the household, be sure to seek out toddler-sized two-piece racing pajama sets or children's sized driver uniforms complete with racing helmets, in addition to the tiny tees and shirts available at your local mall or trackside. No matter how you choose to suit up, with NASCAR attire you'll be sure to find the perfect way to show your fan-affiliation.

Should anybody not be able to find their preferred size or style of NASCAR clothing ready-made, they can always buy 100% cotton NASCAR fabric and make their own clothes. So far there aren't any NASCAR-themed sewing machines on the market, but in a pinch you can always use a few readily available NASCAR stickers to decorate a sewing machine you already have at home!

No Place Like Home

For the truly die-hard NASCAR fan, your favorite sport and your favorite driver can become your home-decorating motif! Fans of a new or relatively unknown driver may have to settle for a couple of posters with their driver's car or picture on it, but those who follow popular, well-established drivers like Mark Martin, Jeff Gordon or Terry Labonte will have no problem furnishing a house (or at least a small apartment) with driver-themed NASCAR products.

Furniture is integral to any decorating scheme and there's plenty of it to be found. Inflatable chairs with the signatures and numbers of drivers like Dale Earnhardt are available in both adult and child sizes and for the adult models you can choose not only which driver you want for your chair, but also if you want a chair shaped like a traditional armchair or a racing seat with tires for armrests.

Driver-inspired floor coverings are also available, ranging from throw rugs to full carpeting. For added effect, try complementing your carpet scheme with wallpaper borders featuring the same driver. And don't forget lighting! The question is not whether you can get a driver-inspired lamp but what sort of lamp you should choose – a car-shaped nightlight whose whole body glows, a car-shaped lamp with light shining from the headlight, a traditional lamp with a car-shaped base or a light fixture decorated with the driver's signature that attaches directly into the ceiling. Should you choose the ceiling light, you can turn it on with a wall switch plate that features a bird's-eye view of the car of your choice.

In the kitchen, you can set your table with driver-licensed stoneware dinner sets and drink out of a variety of driver – or NASCAR – cups, mugs and drink holders. You can also find tabletop or wall-mounted telephones shaped like your favorite driver's car, in addition to TV remote controls and clock radios. Of course, if you feel that you'd like a break from the constant display of cars, you can replace your car-shaped phone with one shaped like a transporter.

For the bedroom, there's no shortage of quilts, afghans, pillow shams and sheet sets with either NASCAR or driver logos. And if the weather's too hot for a lot of bedding, turn on your black ceiling fan with the colorful NASCAR logo on each blade. On your bedside table you might keep your driver's signature alarm clock and, purely for decorative purposes, you set-up the inflatable scale-model race car in the corner of your room which is a perfect match to the three-foot plastic replica you can buy to display on your lawn outside.

Your outdoor decor could also include a NASCAR welcome mat and you can even get a postmaster-approved mailbox with driver numbers and insignia (although the little mailbox flag is the standard red one, not black-and-white checkered – sorry!). To find out about these and many other exciting NASCAR home-decorating tips, check any NASCAR store or web site. CheckerBee's web site, ***CollectorsQuest.com***, also provides feature articles about exciting new product lines that NASCAR fans won't want to miss.

NASCAR® And The Great Outdoors

NASCAR, of course, is an outdoor sport, so it's no surprise that many of its licensed products are intended for outdoor use. For camping or tailgate parties, IntraShade makes waterproof outdoor canopies with official NASCAR or driver logos. Once the canopy has been set up, a few ultra-light folding chairs with your favorite driver's insignia provides a pleasant way to sit in the shade.

Coolers and insulated duffel bags keep drinks cold when they're carried to the races and driver-logo superscopes or binoculars give fans in the grandstands an up-close look at the action on the track. Fans can also snap action photos using 35-millimeter race cameras shaped like their favorite driver's cars.

Hopefully the race won't be rained out, but maybe you should take your NASCAR plastic rain poncho or NASCAR umbrella just in case. Enjoy the race!

Die-Cast Differences

Over the past several years, NASCAR collectibles have progressed under the careful supervision of the many die-cast manufacturers. Always striving to ensure that the highest level of collectibility is achieved, as well as complete customer satisfaction, die-cast manufacturers are constantly looking for ways to increase the realism of the cars by adding as many details as possible. So, as manufacturers work to achieve the look and feel of a real NASCAR race car, all the while supplying cars to market soon after their debut on the racetrack, they are looking for ways to perfect what was already a very difficult production process.

However, it is important to remember that no matter how advanced the technology becomes, there will always be a certain percentage of differences between the car you display in your living room and the real car you'll find displayed at the track. The same also holds true between the car you display in your living room and the car your neighbor displays in his living room. The reason being, as you'll find in many different genres of collectibles, variations (pieces that have color, design or printed changes from the "original" piece) often make their way to store shelves even though manufacturers attempt to maintain the highest standards of quality control.

A variation, however, is not necessarily a bad thing. Quite often collectors seek out these "oddities" in order to add a rare or unique piece to their collection. In fact, variations sometimes will result in a piece having a higher value on the secondary market (perhaps even tremendously so) as collectors relish the thought of having such a limited piece of die-cast in their NASCAR collection.

Cars may also differ in appearance due to instructions from the manufacturer. Based on the amount of supplies or innovations in technology, the manufacturer will sometimes order changes to the car midway through a production run.

Due to both intentional factory changes and human error, there is an extremely large number of variations. Common variations involve changes in body style, sponsor logos, wheels and tires or packaging.

Body Style

Due to advancing technology and innovative new designs, the body styles of race cars have changed significantly over the years. In turn, so have the body styles of their die-cast replicas. Generally speaking, a change in body style will not occur in the middle of a production run, but when this does happen it causes a very noticeable variation within the line.

One of the easiest ways to spot a body style variation is to look at the size of the grill openings on the front of the car. Older models tend to have smaller openings, while newer replicas have larger, more defined openings. Similarly, rear window straps can often be found on cars before 1992, while later versions do not include this detail. Roof rails, however, were added to these newer models, giving collectors an easy way to identify the approximate age of their model car. Models changed once again in the mid-1990s, as detailed headlights and fog lights were added to the race car replicas to give them a more realistic look.

Sponsor Logos

Primary sponsor logos, located on the hood of the car, are also subject to variations. The 1995 Action 1:24 scale replica of the Winston Silver Select driven by Dale Earnhardt was painted in two ways: 10,000 models were painted with the word "parts" on the hood while 500 were released without it.

Sponsor logos are printed onto the die-cast replicas through a process known as tampo printing. Tampo printing, or tampo painting as it is sometimes called, is a screen printing process which is somewhat similar to rubber stamping. This process is very accurate and eliminates the need for hand painting, thus reducing the possible margin of human error. However, if die-cast models are not kept in the same position during the tampo printing process by machine operators, there will be a distinct variation between the original car and the replica.

Wheels And Tires

Over the years, several styles of wheels have been featured on die-cast models. Removable rubber tires were featured on earlier versions of Racing Champions cars, but in 1990, Racing Champions started using non-removable plastic tires (though some 1990 cars still had tires made of rubber). Another version of plastic tires surfaced in the line in 1992, when "Goodyear Eagle" replaced "Racing Champions" on the surface of the tire.

Hot Wheels is another die-cast manufacturer that has featured a number of tire variations over the years. Although variations of the tires, wheels, hubs and spokes can all be found on different models of Hot Wheels vehicles over the years, most NASCAR models can be found with one of two major tire variations. Pro Circuit models, which made their debut in 1992, feature plastic wheels and plastic tires and can be found with large spokes in various colors. A second version of race car tires also made its way onto Hot Wheels NASCAR replicas in 1992. These feature rubber tires and gray or chrome hubs which are highlighted by five bolts through the center. Both of these versions can be found on the models that are produced by Hot Wheels today.

Depending on the line and model that you buy, you are bound to find a wheel or tire variation of one type or another. Common variations include the color of the car's hubs, which may vary from white to gray to yellow. In addition, spokes and redlines may or may not be found on the tires.

Packaging

Packaging is considered as much a part of the collectible as the die-cast car itself, so it should come as no surprise that variations in a die-cast model's packaging hold just as much importance to collectors as do variations on the vehicle.

Die-cast cars are usually packaged in either a box or a blister pack and some manufacturers have been known to package cars in both, leading to yet another variation within the line. Spelling errors may also occur on the packaging. For instance, collectors who purchased a 1998 Dale Earnhardt Jr. Revell 1:24 or 1:18 car most likely received the piece in a box that had Earnhardt Jr.'s name misspelled.

While there are several variations in existence, only a few of them carry a significant secondary market value. Sometimes when the variation makes the die-cast car a less-than-accurate version of the original, the variation will actually decrease the value of the piece rather than increase its worth. So if you do happen to find a unique variation, you may be better off holding on to the piece for the sentimental value rather than trying to sell it for a hefty profit.

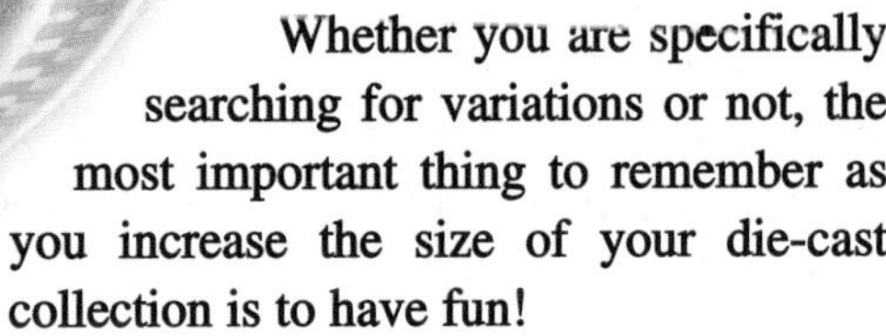

Whether you are specifically searching for variations or not, the most important thing to remember as you increase the size of your die-cast collection is to have fun!

The Making Of A Die-Cast Collectible

Creating die-cast models of a NASCAR stock car goes far beyond the act of pouring molten metal into a cast. As NASCAR fans only want the most accurate depiction of their favorite driver's race car, a lot of effort is put into the detail of the car by the different die-cast manufacturers Special attention is paid to every aspect of the car's presentation and manufacturers work with both the drivers and their teams to ensure that the intricate paint jobs and special decals are accurately represented.

The die-cast process first begins with the manufacturer obtaining approval to reproduce the car. Once the necessary legal permissions have been granted, the first step in creating a die-cast replica is to capture the image of the car on film or paper. If the design is based on an existing automobile, pictures of the car are taken from several angles to ensure accuracy. The photographers pay special attention to the car's interior as well as the exterior and often take several photos of the dash and engine.

Die-cast manufacturers continue to work with the drivers, car owners and automotive manufacturers to get information on the specific model of car that the driver uses. In addition, measurements are often taken so that the miniature replica resembles the original as accurately as possible.

As the production process begins, molds are created which are based on the drawings and photographs of the original cars. Each part of the car is divided up and molded individually. A completed model car can consist of up to 100 different molds, including the undercarriage, hood and body.

Molten metal is then poured into each of the molds to form the shape of the car. It is not unusual for several similar cars to be produced from the same molds. In fact, some companies only use three or four different molds based on the types of cars involved in stock car racing. Jeff Gordon's DuPont car might be made out of the same mold as Dale Earnhardt Jr.'s Budweiser car, since they are both Chevrolet Monte Carlos.

After the cast is made, the individual parts of the car are then ready to be painted. A base color is first used, which is then baked onto the car to ensure the paint will adhere. The base color is always the most prominent color to be featured on the car, while the other colors, as well as sponsor logos, are applied later in a process called tampo printing.

Tampo printing is the process of applying colored dies over the base coat to form the sponsors' insignias and any other designs found on the car. The dies are currently applied by machine rather than the former process of applying by hand, which allows time to be saved and also allows less room for error. However, factory operators must still be very careful to make sure that all cars are placed in the same position on the machine so that they are printed in exactly the same place. Tampo printing is not used by all manufacturers, however, some companies opt to have their die-cast replicas spray-painted instead.

After the pieces of the die-cast car are painted, the sections of the replica are then assembled. Finally, at the end of the production process, the tires and other plastic parts, like the window screen, are added.

While there are many different manufacturers of die-cast cars, most models are packaged in one of two ways. Larger models, such as 1:24 and 1:18 scale, are sold in cardboard boxes, the color and design of which varies from manufacturer to manufacturer. Smaller scale models such as 1:64 come in blister packs, which are plastic bubbles that are attached to a cardboard backing. No matter what type of packaging is used or what manufacturer produced the car, you will always find some form of printed information on the packaging that pertains to the specific piece.

With such a wide variety of scales and styles available in the world of die-cast racing collectibles, prices can run anywhere from under $10 to several hundred dollars. Expect to pay anywhere from $4 to $150 at retail for a typical die-cast piece, but keep in mind that several factors influence the price including the scale, manufacturer and quantity scheduled to be produced.

Terms To Know To Sound Like A Pro

aerodynamics – the study of air flow and how its resistance and pressure will be affected by the speed, shape and movement of a race car.

associate sponsor – an individual or business that helps finance a driver or team. Though these sponsors cannot advertise on the hood of the car, they can place their logos on the side of the car and the driver's uniform.

chassis – the steel frame of a race car.

checkered flag – signifies the end of a race.

compression ratio – the amount that the air and fuel within the engine is compressed. A higher compression generates more horsepower.

contingency programs – promotions run by sponsors to further advertise their product. During a contingency program, a driver may be awarded a special bonus by a sponsor if he has that sponsor's decal on his car when he runs the race.

crew chief – the crew chief is responsible for the performance of the race car and all actions of his pit crew. He decides when the driver should pit and what repairs need to be made, as well as making sure that the car passes all inspections.

die-cast – a scale-model car formed by pouring molten metal into special casts, letting it cool, then painting it to look like an existing car.

drafting – a technique drivers use to increase speed and conserve gasoline. When one car closely follows another at high speeds, the second car gets sucked into the vacuum created behind the first car, enabling both to travel faster.

exclusive – a collectible available only through a specific store, company or promotion.

fuel cell – a metal box containing foam padding and an inner tear-resistant pouch to hold gasoline. The fuel cell minimizes spillage in an accident.

happy hour – the last practice before a race begins. It is strictly timed at one hour and is the last time that cars will enter the track before the race begins.

hat dance – a photo opportunity held at the end of a race, when a driver puts on a series of hats (one from each of his sponsors) and poses for pictures in them.

hauler – a truck that serves as the race team's "home away from home." The hauler is where the team holds meetings and rests when a race is not ongoing.

hood open – a die-cast collectible created so that its hood can open and close. These models usually include detailed representations of a car's engine.

horsepower – the measurement of power used in stock car racing. One unit of horsepower is the amount needed to move 33,000 pounds at one foot per minute.

loose – when a car's rear wheels are hard to control, making the car more susceptible to spinouts.

NASCAR – acronym for the National Association for Stock Car Auto Racing. NASCAR was developed to unify rules and standards for the sport.

No Bull 5 – A million-dollar bonus program for which drivers become eligible by placing in the top five in one of that season's designated No Bull 5 races. If the eligible driver then wins the next No Bull 5 race, he also wins the million dollars.

pace car – a car which sets the speed for certain parts of the race. When the race is under caution, the cars must follow the speed of the pace car to avoid traveling too fast. The pace car also sets the maximum speed for the pit road.

paint scheme – the colors and designs that decorate a car.

pit road – the stretch of pavement found on the inside of the track where the pit crews are located. It is here that the drivers make pit stops to refuel and repair their cars.

point system – the ratings system that determines the season's series champion. Points are awarded for leading laps and winning races. Whoever holds the most points at the end of the season is that year's Winston Cup Champion.

pole winner – the driver who runs a lap in the shortest amount of time. Also known as the pole sitter, this driver wins the right to choose the position of his pit box and the chance to start the race from the inside front row (which is known as the pole position).

primary sponsor – an individual or business that finances the bulk of the expenses of the race driver and their team in exchange for primary advertising rights on the car. Primary sponsors' names and logos are featured on the hood of the race car.

race purse – the prize money offered to the winner of a race.

restrictor plate – a metal plate with four holes that match up to the four holes of a carburetor. When the restrictor plate is placed on top of a vehicle's carburetor, the holes restrict the flow of fuel, reducing the amount of horsepower needed and, ultimately, slowing the car down to ensure safety.

roll bars – thick steel tubes that make up the roll cage around the driver's seat and help to protect the driver in an accident.

roof flaps – metal flaps that stay down while a car is going forward, but are built to fly up when a car goes in reverse or sideways. Roof flaps are used to prevent the car from becoming airborne if a driver loses control.

rookie – a driver in his first year of Winston Cup racing. Rookies can be recognized by a red stripe on the fender of their cars. Each year, the rookie with the most points at the end of the season is honored with the Rookie Of The Year award.

round of wedge – also known as a "round of bite," this phrase refers to the turning of the car's jacking screws. Each turn of the screw helps to redistribute the weight of the car between the two front tires.

spotter – a member of the driver's team who watches the race from the highest point at the racetrack. Spotters use a radio to communicate with the driver and pit crew, in order to give them warnings and advice about upcoming dangers and situations on the racetrack.

stock car – a specially designed automobile that is loosely based on the models driven on the road today. Stock cars, however, contain many differences from their counterparts available to consumers. Current approved models of stock cars for NASCAR racing include the Chevrolet Monte Carlo, Pontiac Grand Prix and Ford Taurus, while the Dodge Intrepid will be added to the list in 2001. These cars have no doors or headlights and a unique interior which protects drivers from the dangers of driving at high speeds.

superspeedway – a track that is over two miles long and requires the use of restrictor plates on carburetors. Currently, Daytona and Talladega are the only two Winston Cup tracks to be considered superspeedways.

tachometer – a device which measures the engine's number of revolutions per minute. The tachometer is used to tell how hard the engine is working.

tight – a car whose front wheels are hard to operate, making turns difficult to navigate.

Victory Lane – a private area where drivers and their pit crews, families and friends can gather to celebrate their victory after a race. The media is also welcome in this area.

Winston Cup Series – NASCAR's most elite stock car racing division.

The Winston Million – a promotion run by sponsor R.J. Reynolds in which any driver who wins three out of four major races, including the Winston 500 at Talledega, the Southern 500 at Darlington, the World 600 at Charlotte and the Daytona 500 wins a $1 million bonus. The program was discontinued in 1997 and replaced by the No Bull 5 promotion. Bill Elliott and Jeff Gordon were the only Winston Million winners.

Alphabetical Index

– Key –

All die-cast cars are listed below in alphabetical order by year. The first number refers to the piece's page within the Value Guide section and the second to the box in which it is pictured on that page.

Acknowledgements

CheckerBee Publishing would like to extend a special thanks to Mark A. Cassidy; Donald Britt; Pauline Caudill; Cyndy Norton; Charles Ross; Bill Grey and Violet Posci at Race World; Bruce Breton and Dave Daniels at Collectibles of Auto Racing; Emile at Catch the Wave; Marcel Gagnon at Diamond 4; Dave at Dave's Racing Collectibles and J.D. and Doug of Carmen's Diecast. These individuals all contributed their valuable time to assist us with this book.